Finding a Safe Place from Abuse

Sheila Hollins, Patricia Scotland and
Noëlle Blackman
illustrated by Anne-Marie Perks

Beyond Words

London

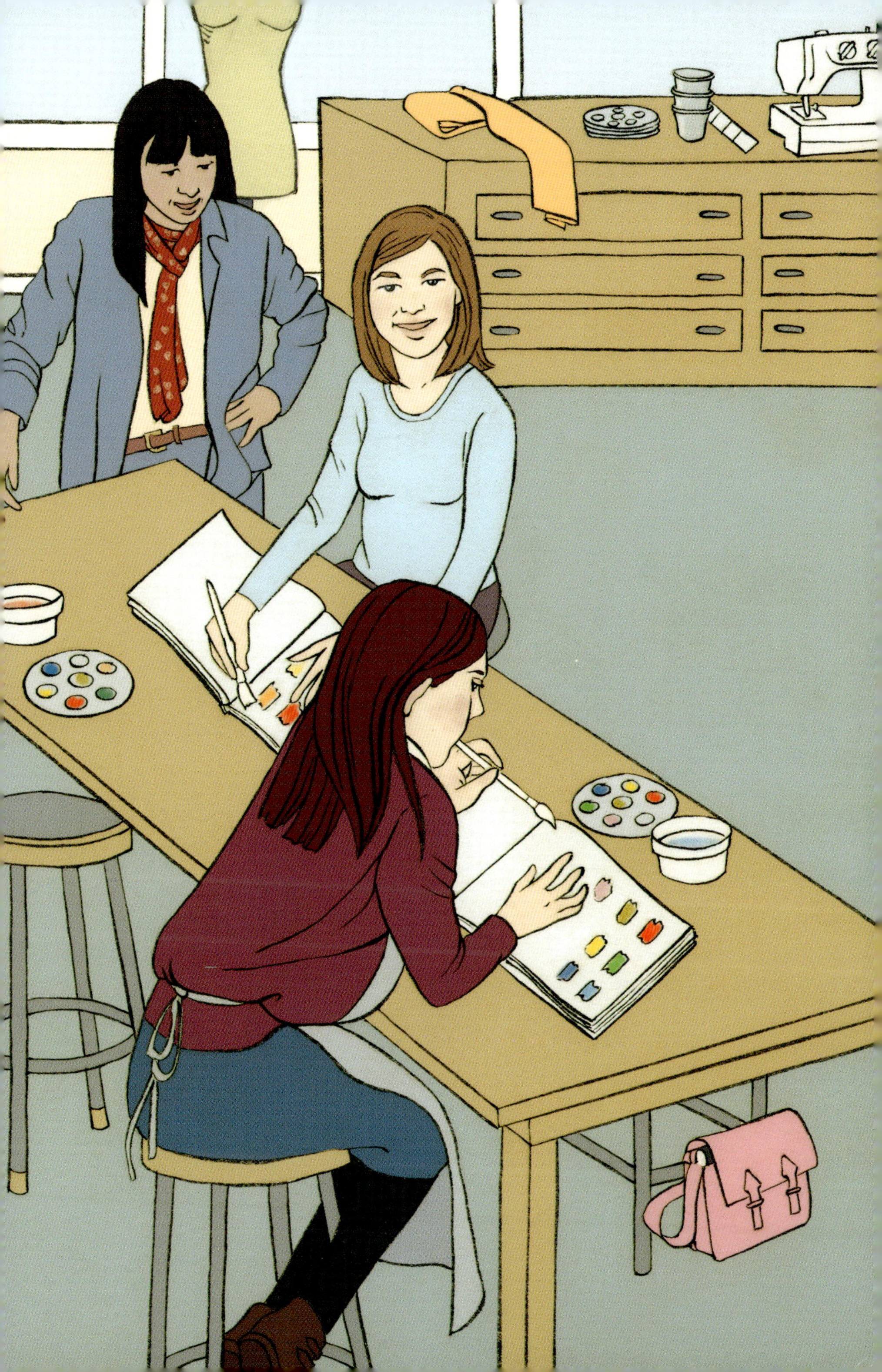

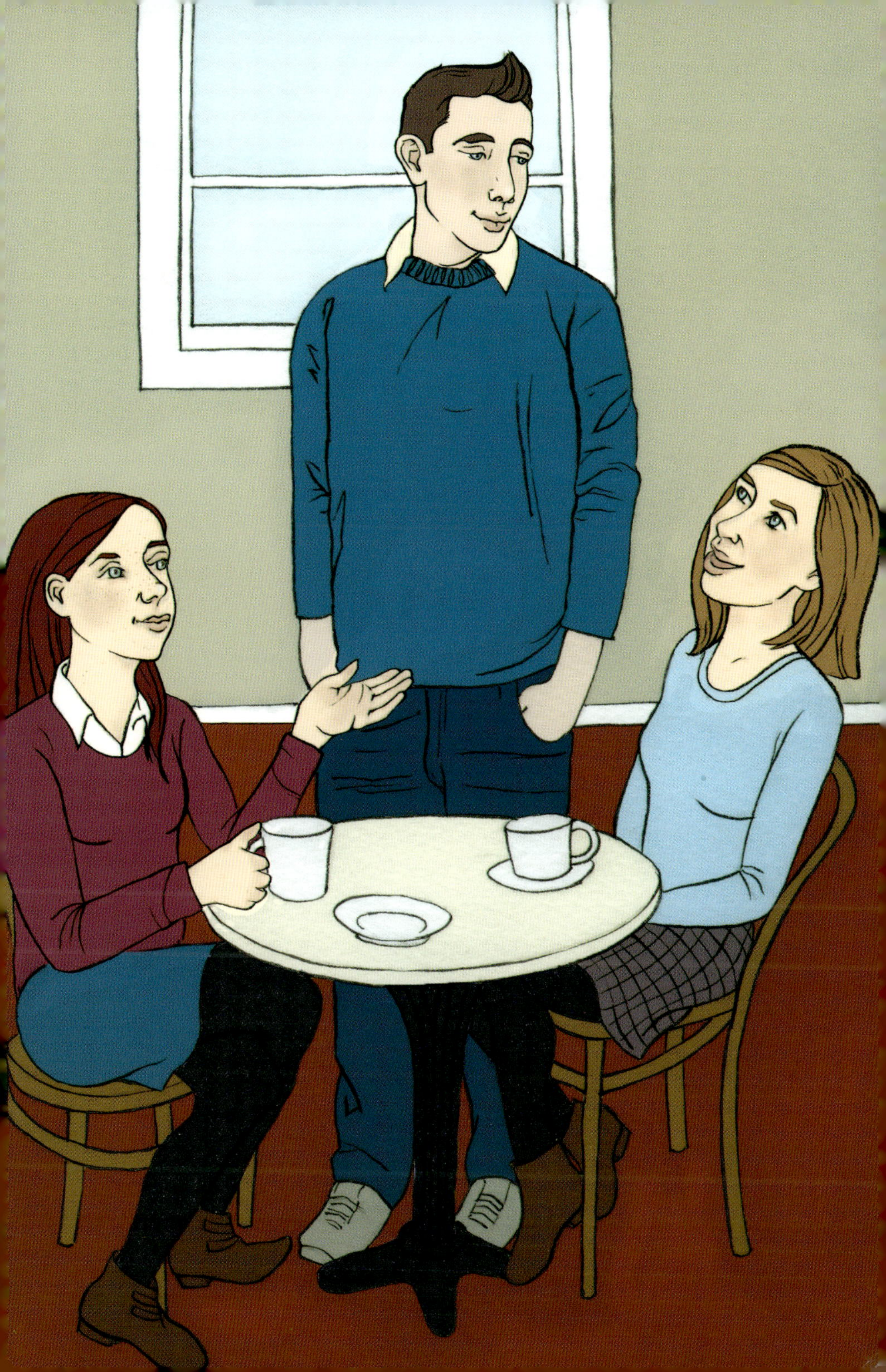

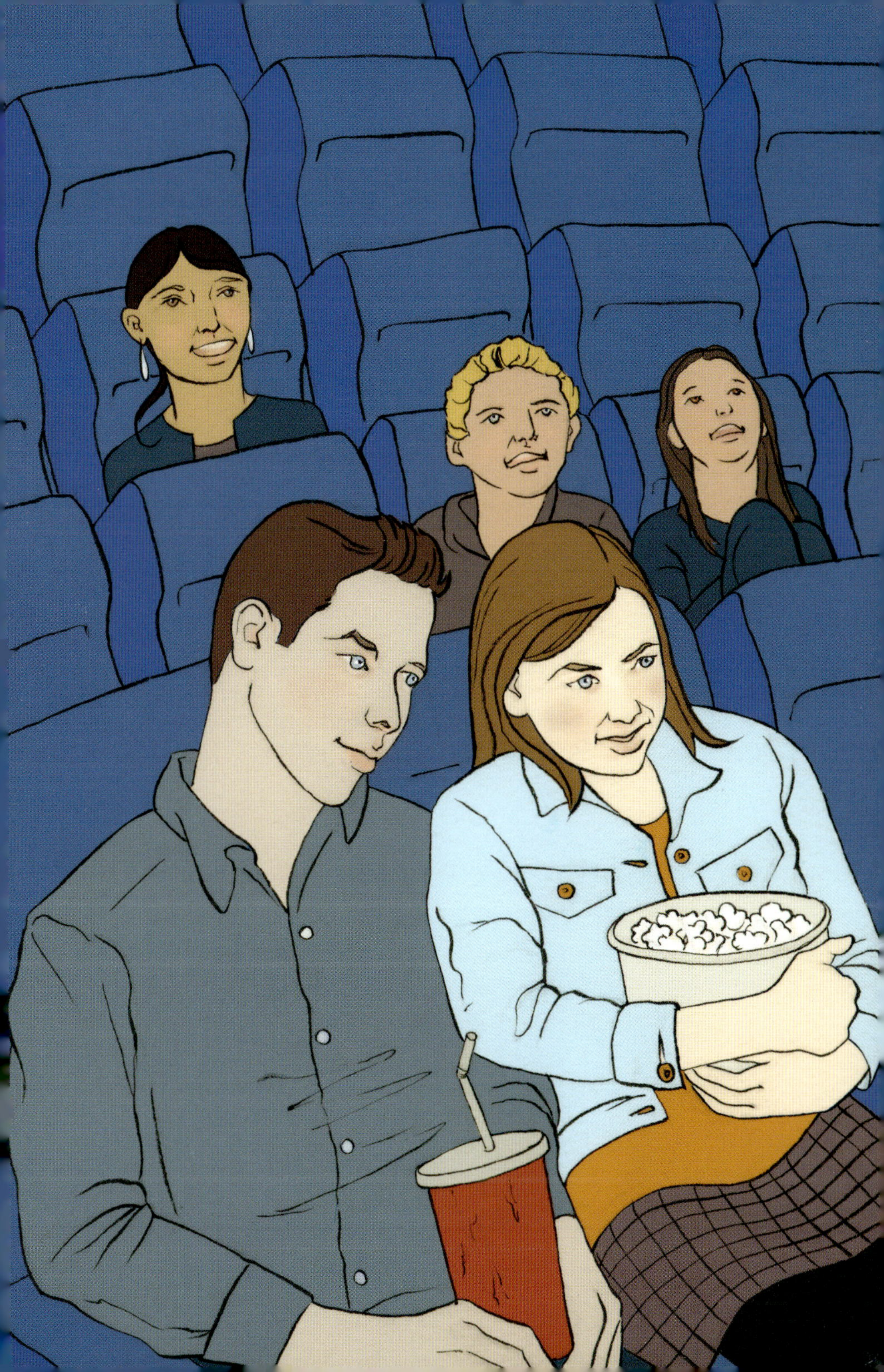

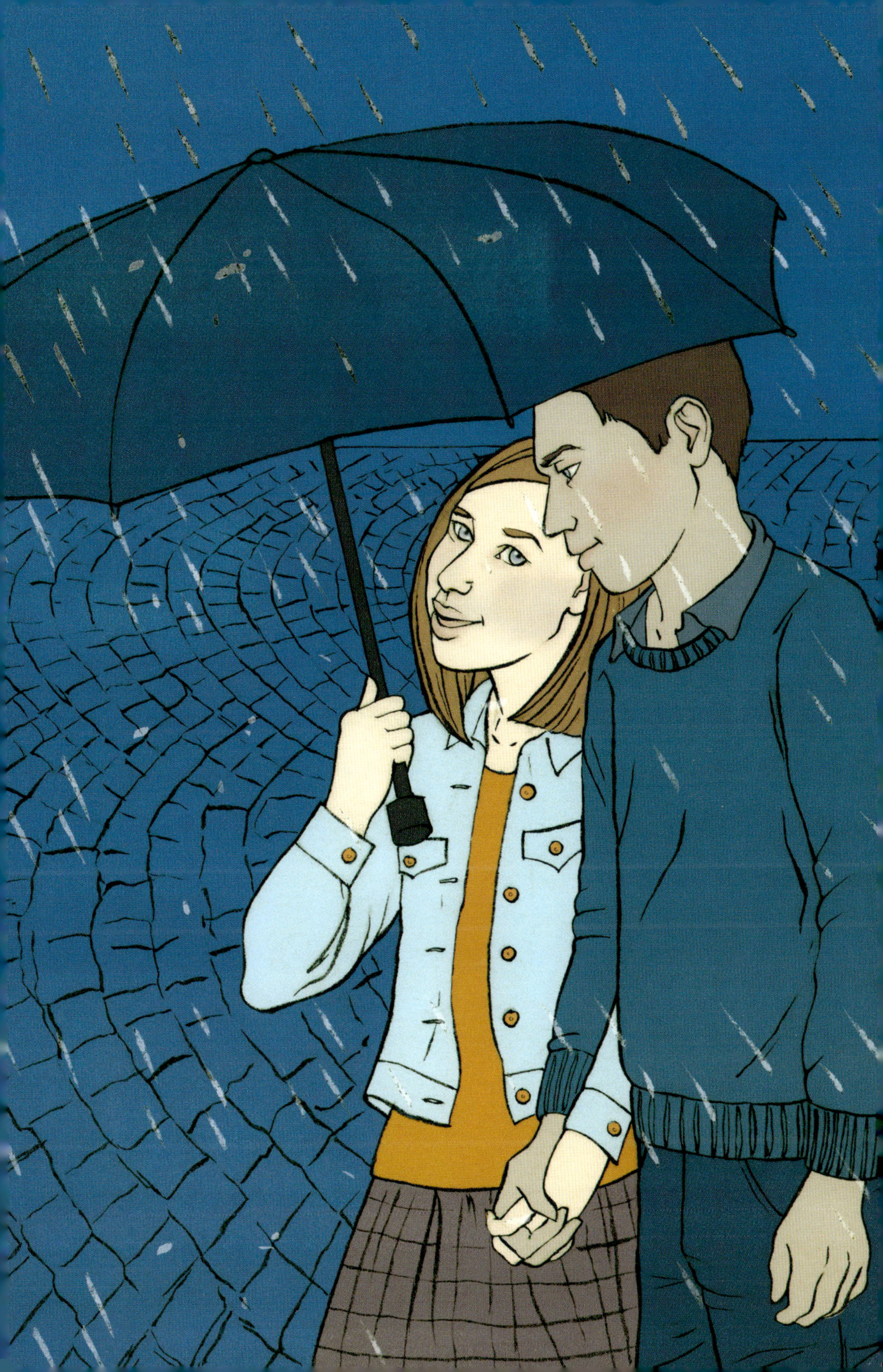

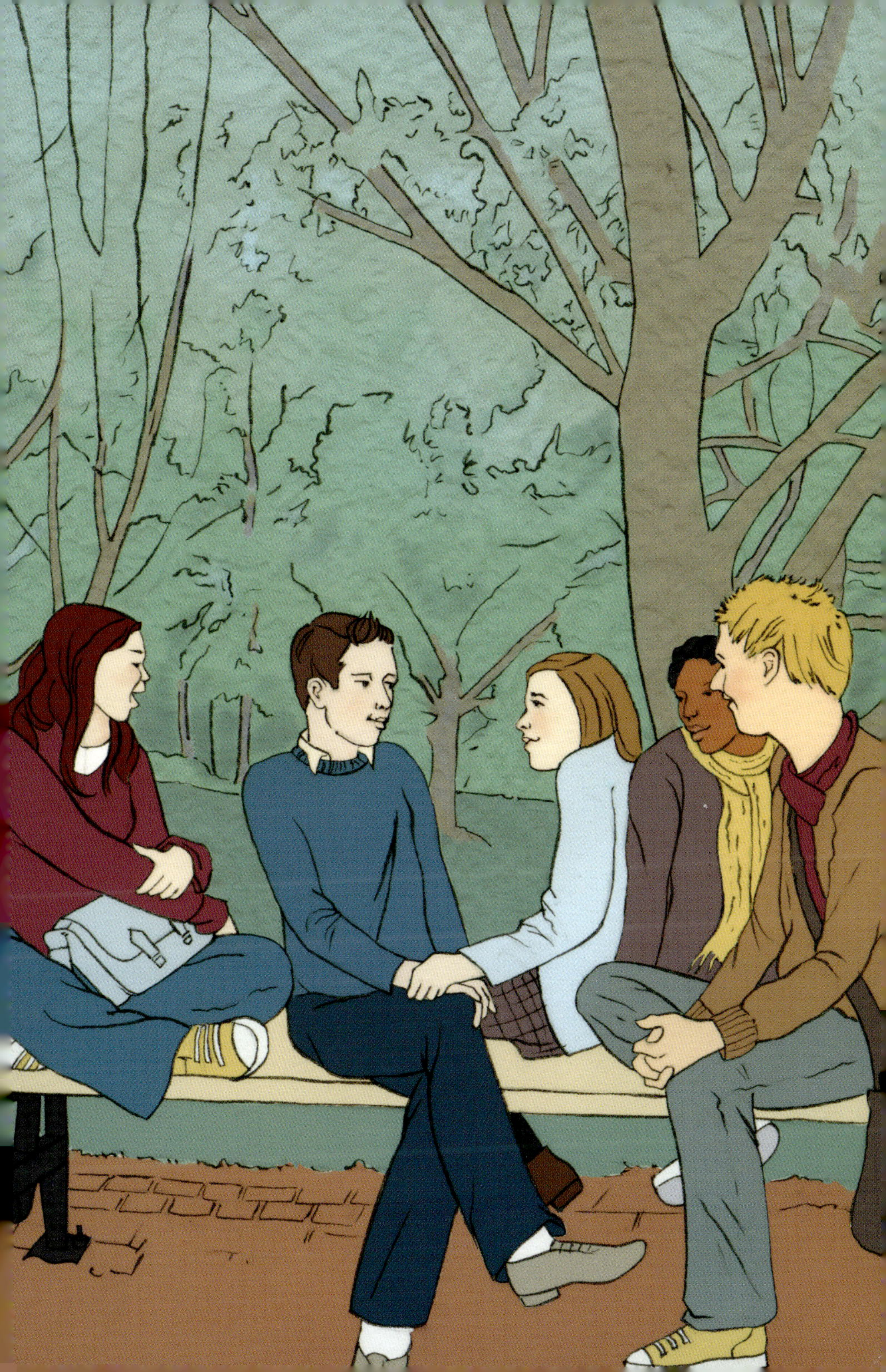

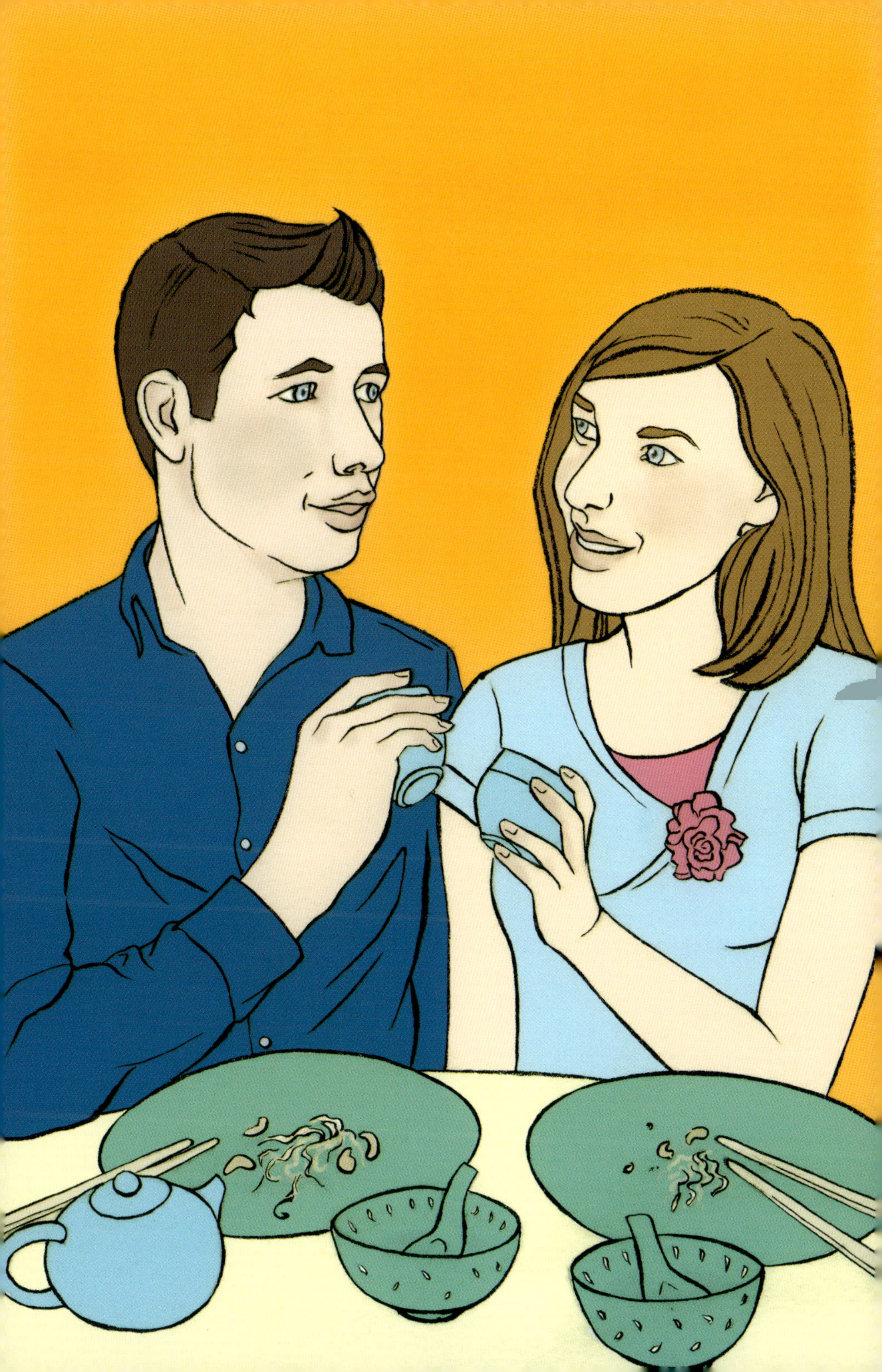

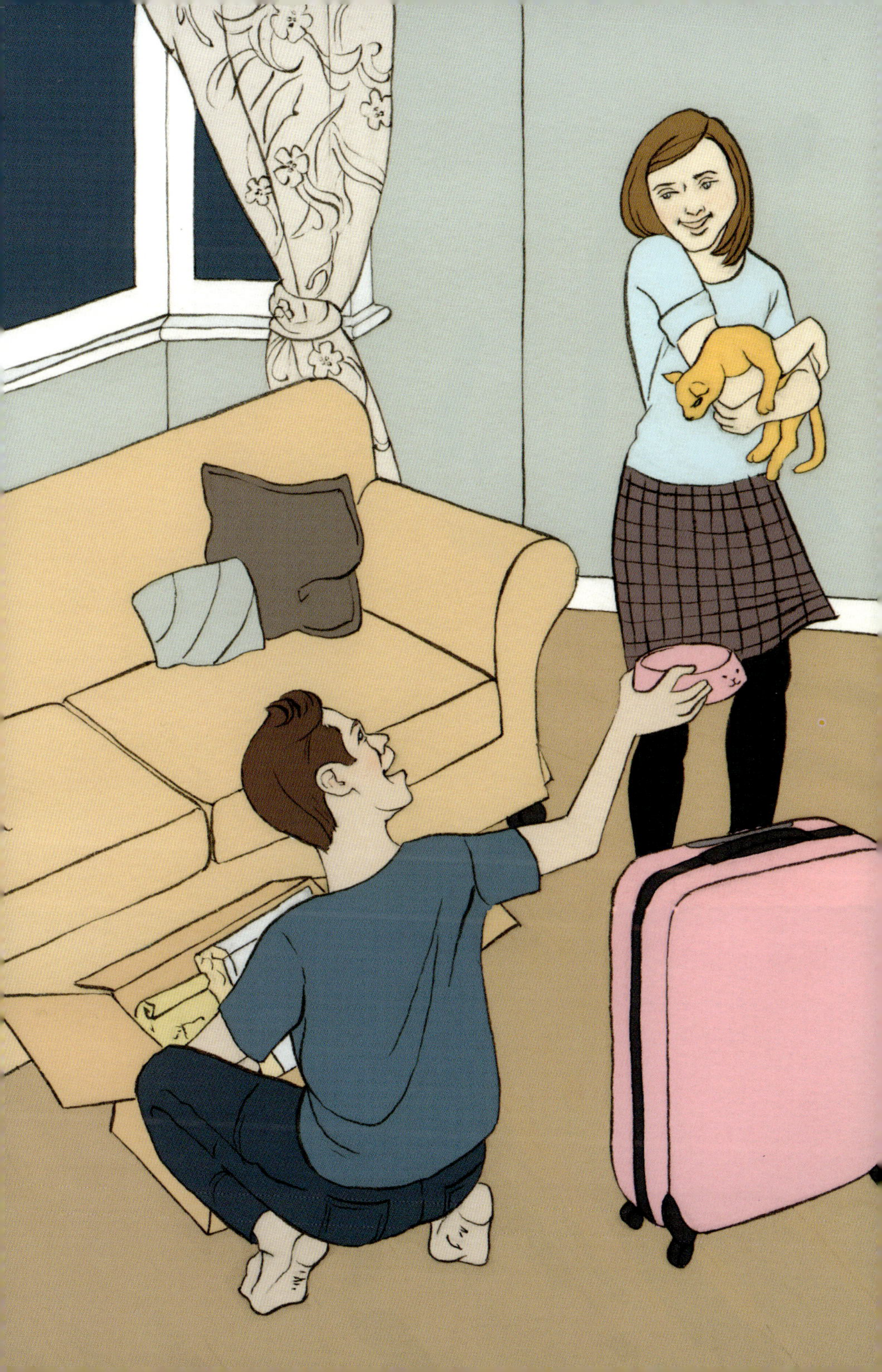

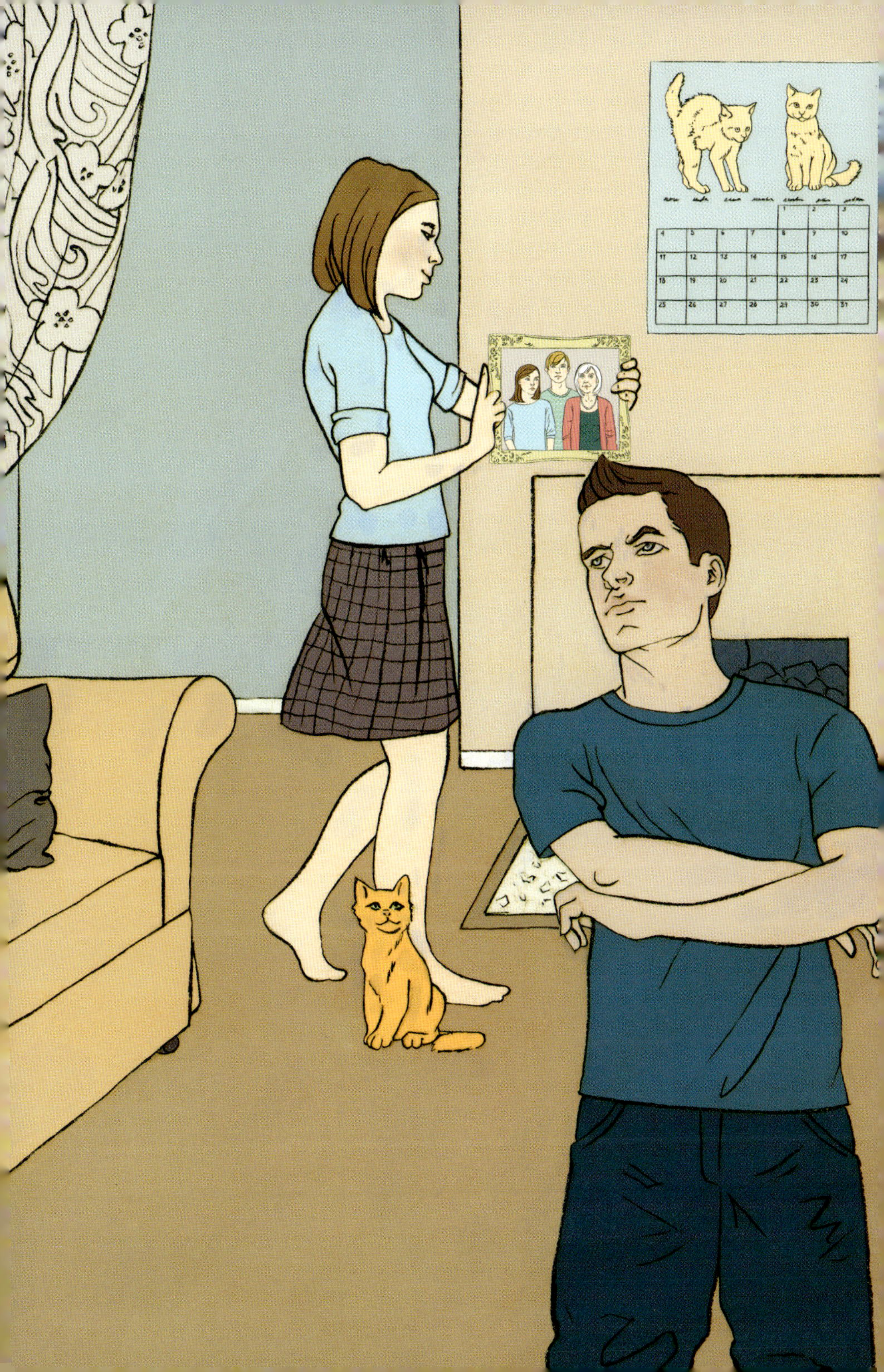

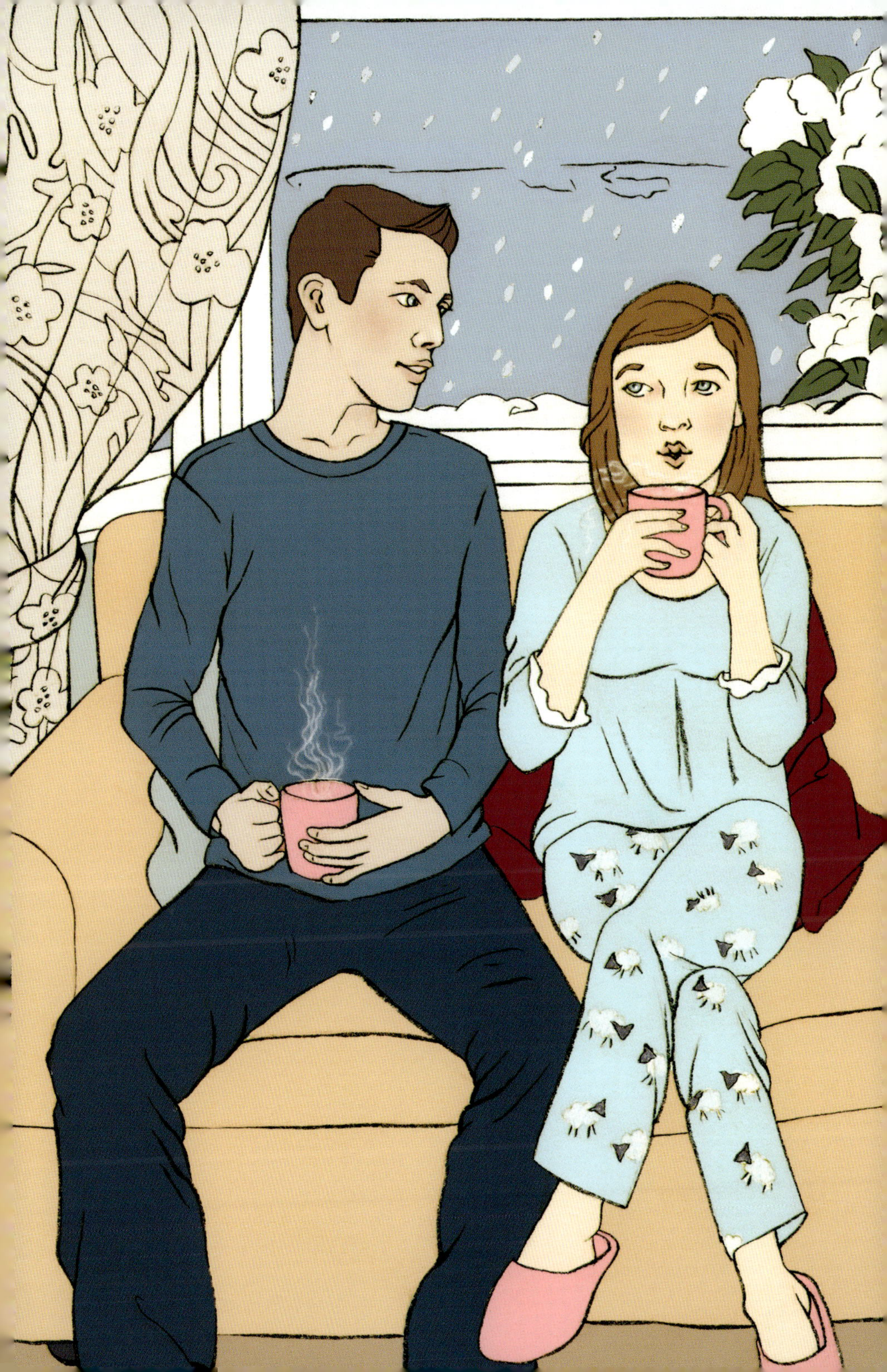

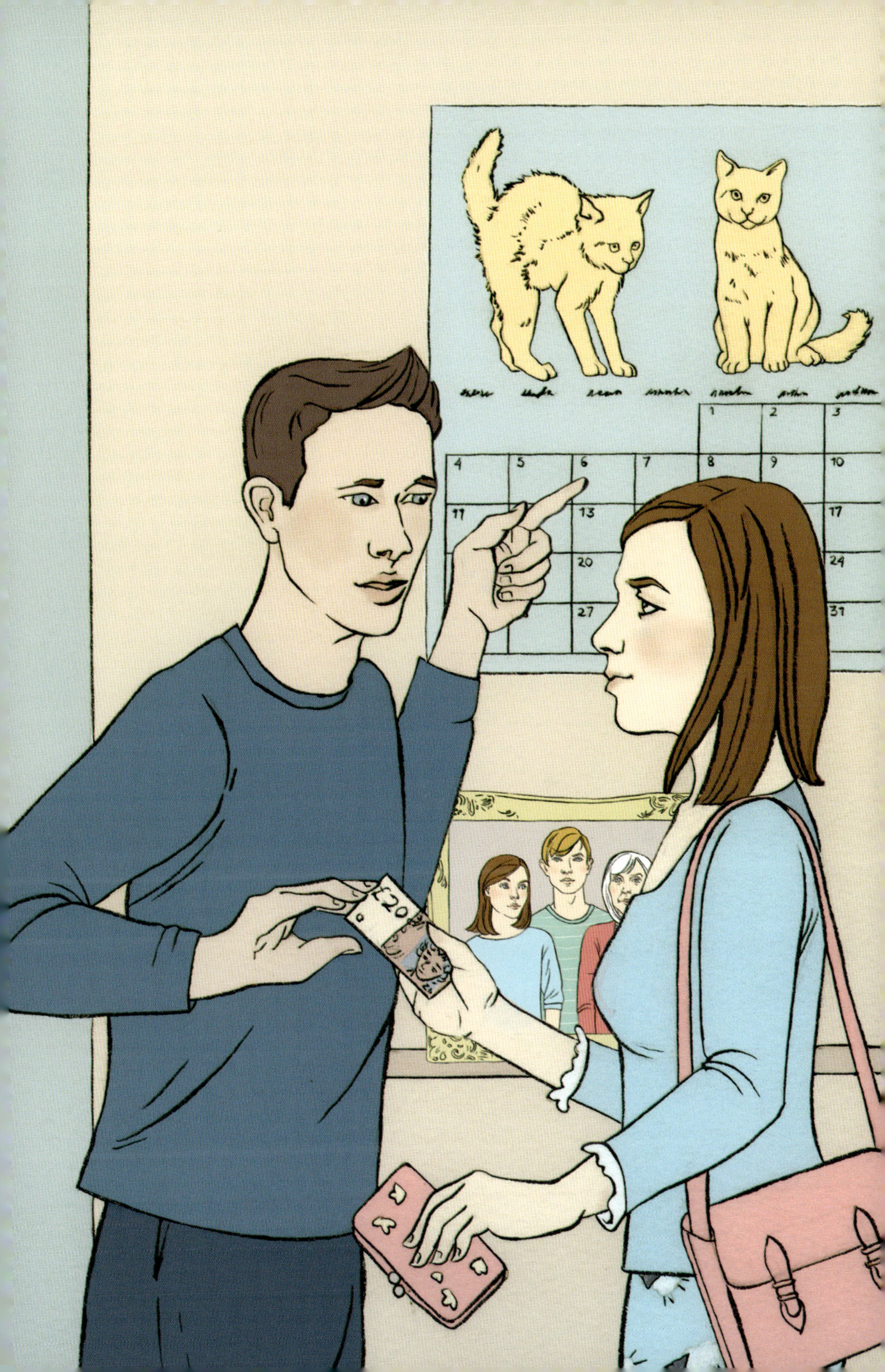

1 2 3
4 5 6 7 8 9 10
11 13 17
20 24
27 31
£20

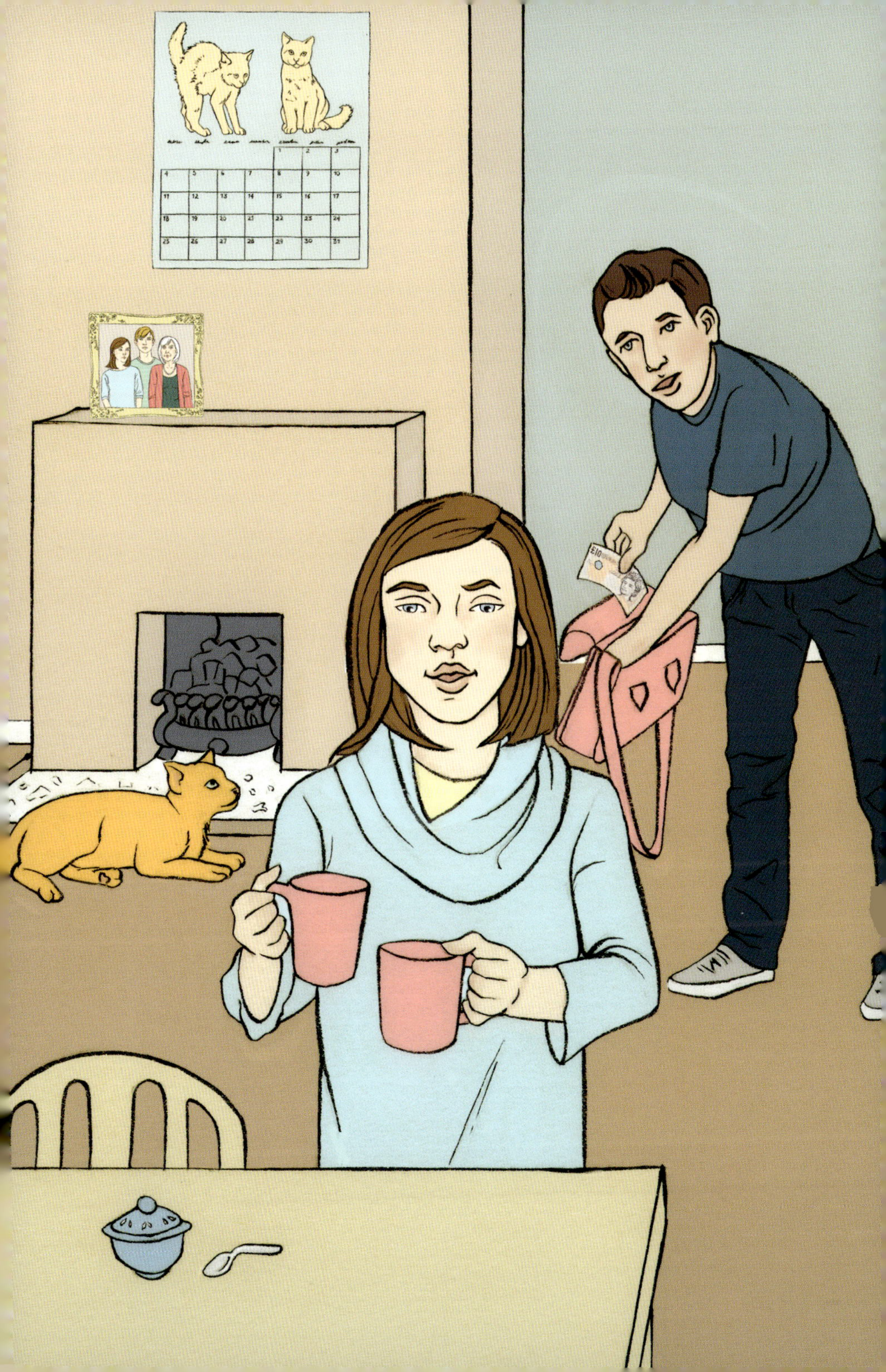

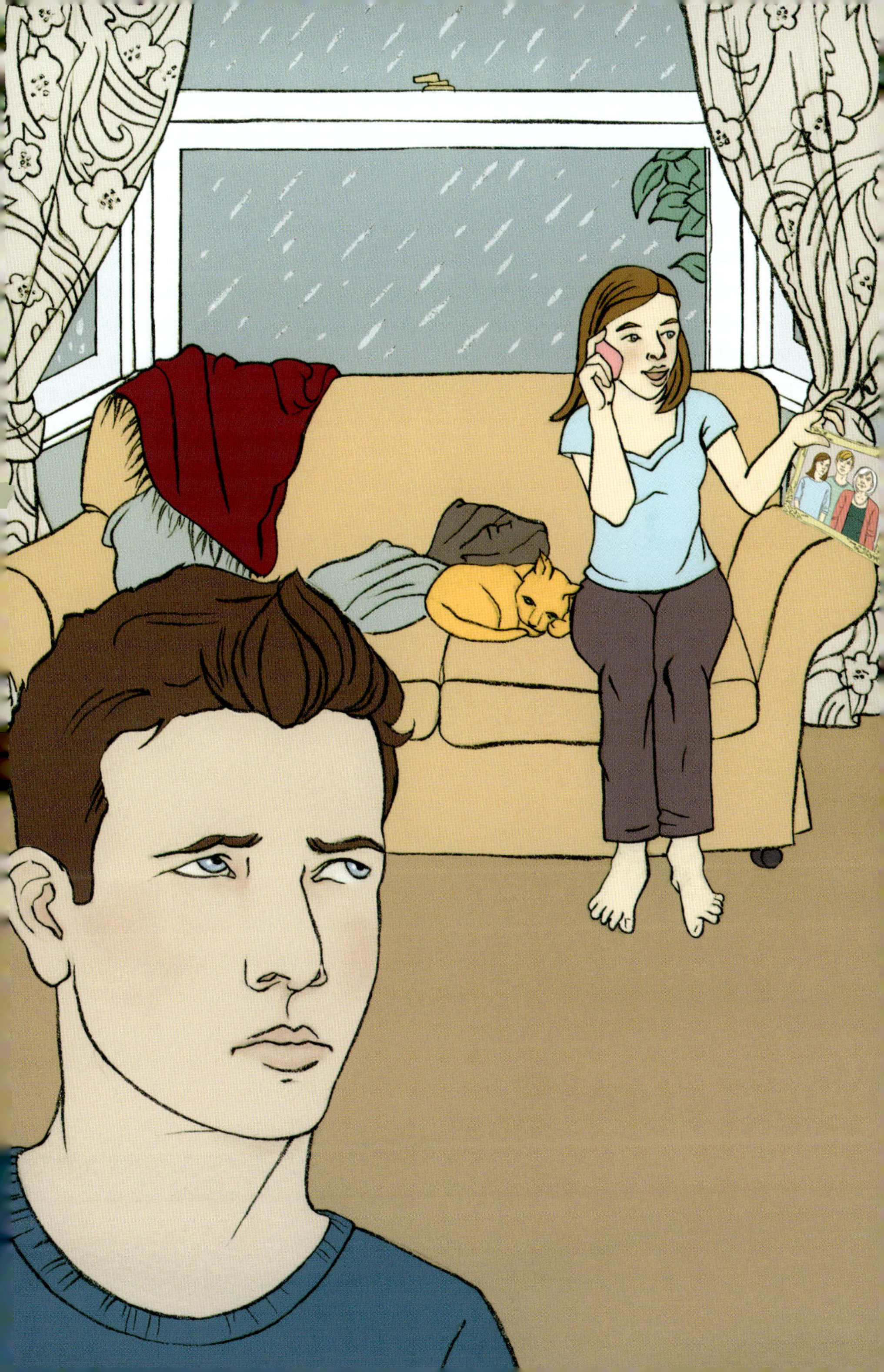

14

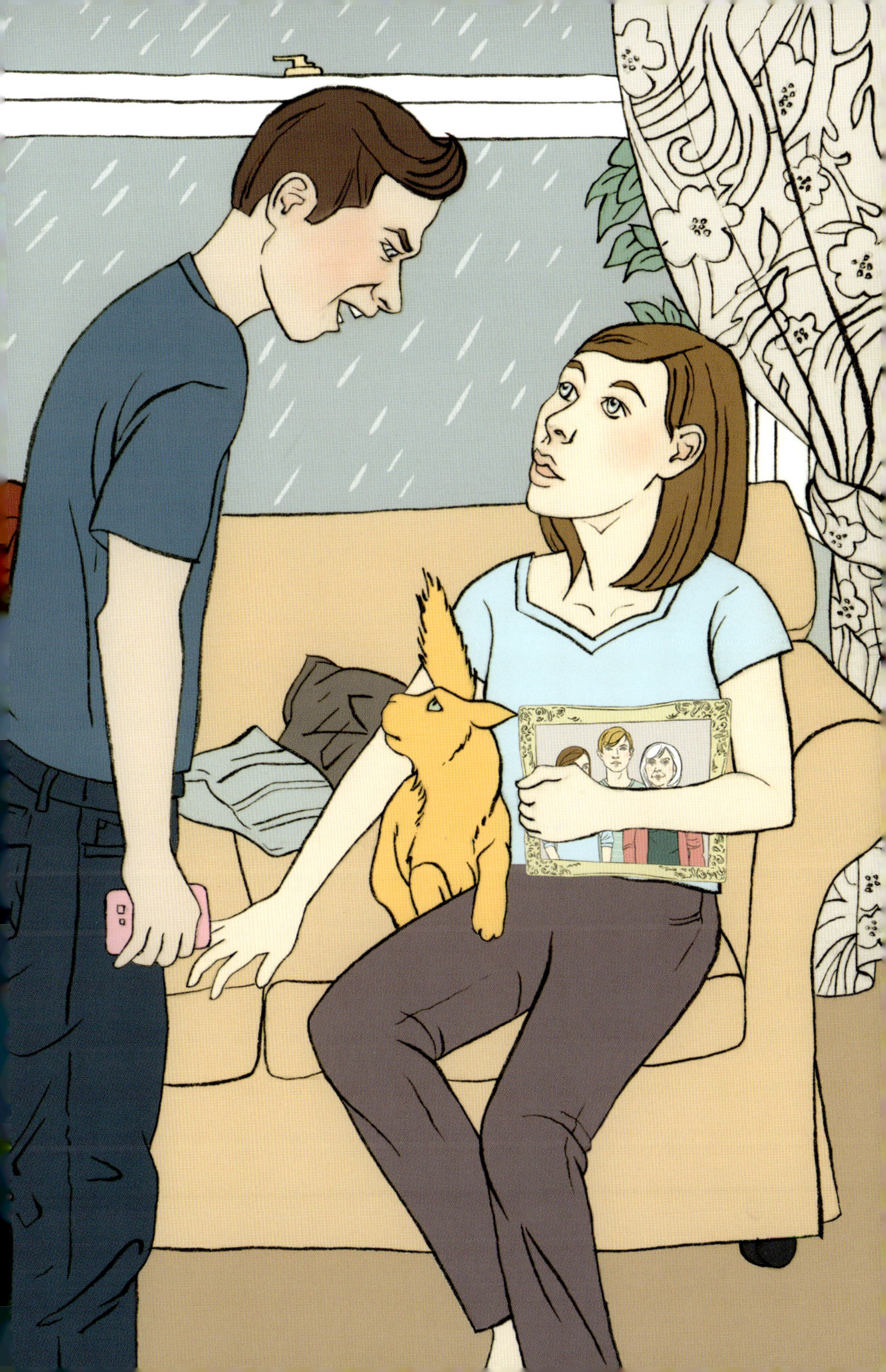

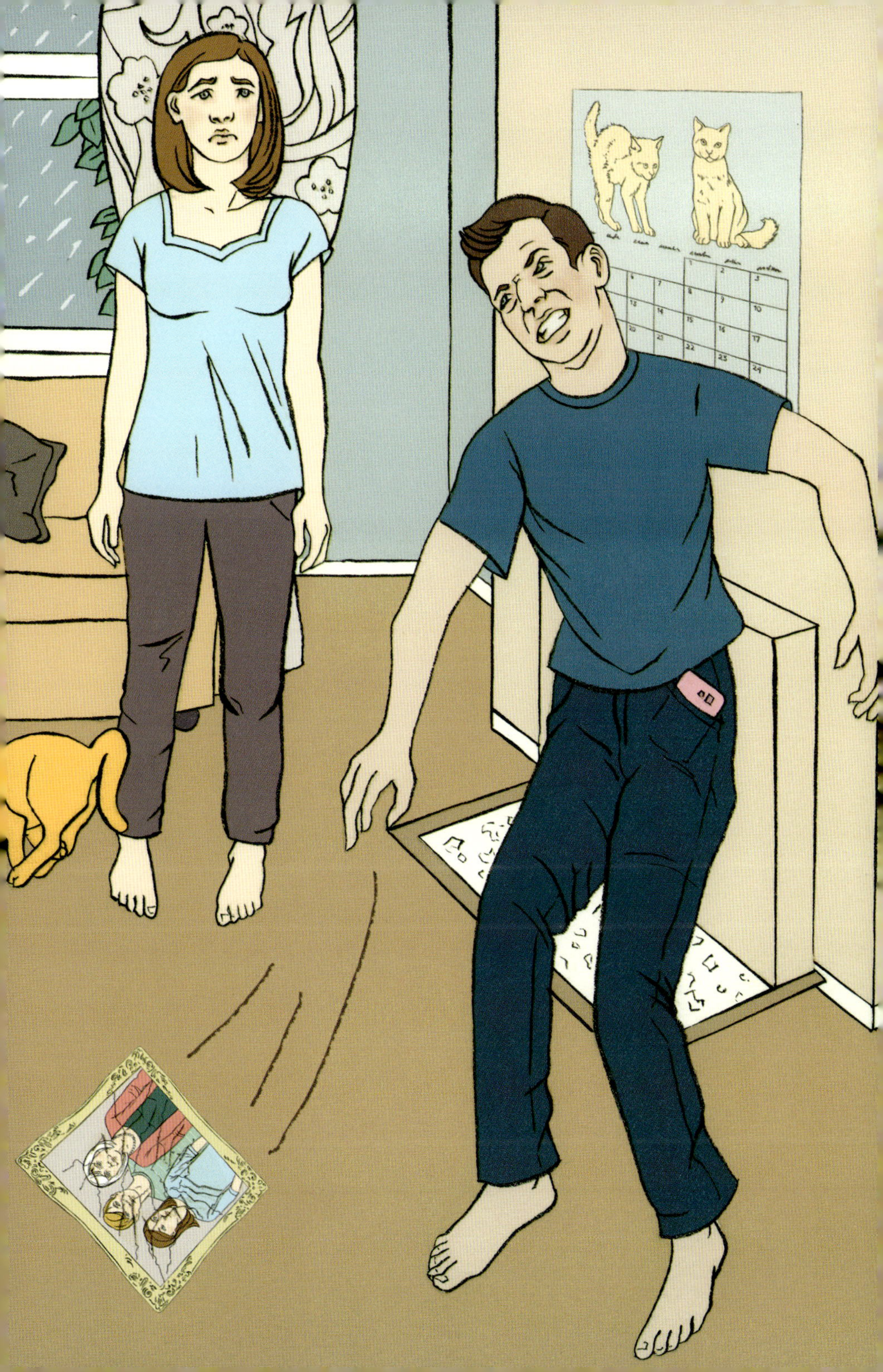

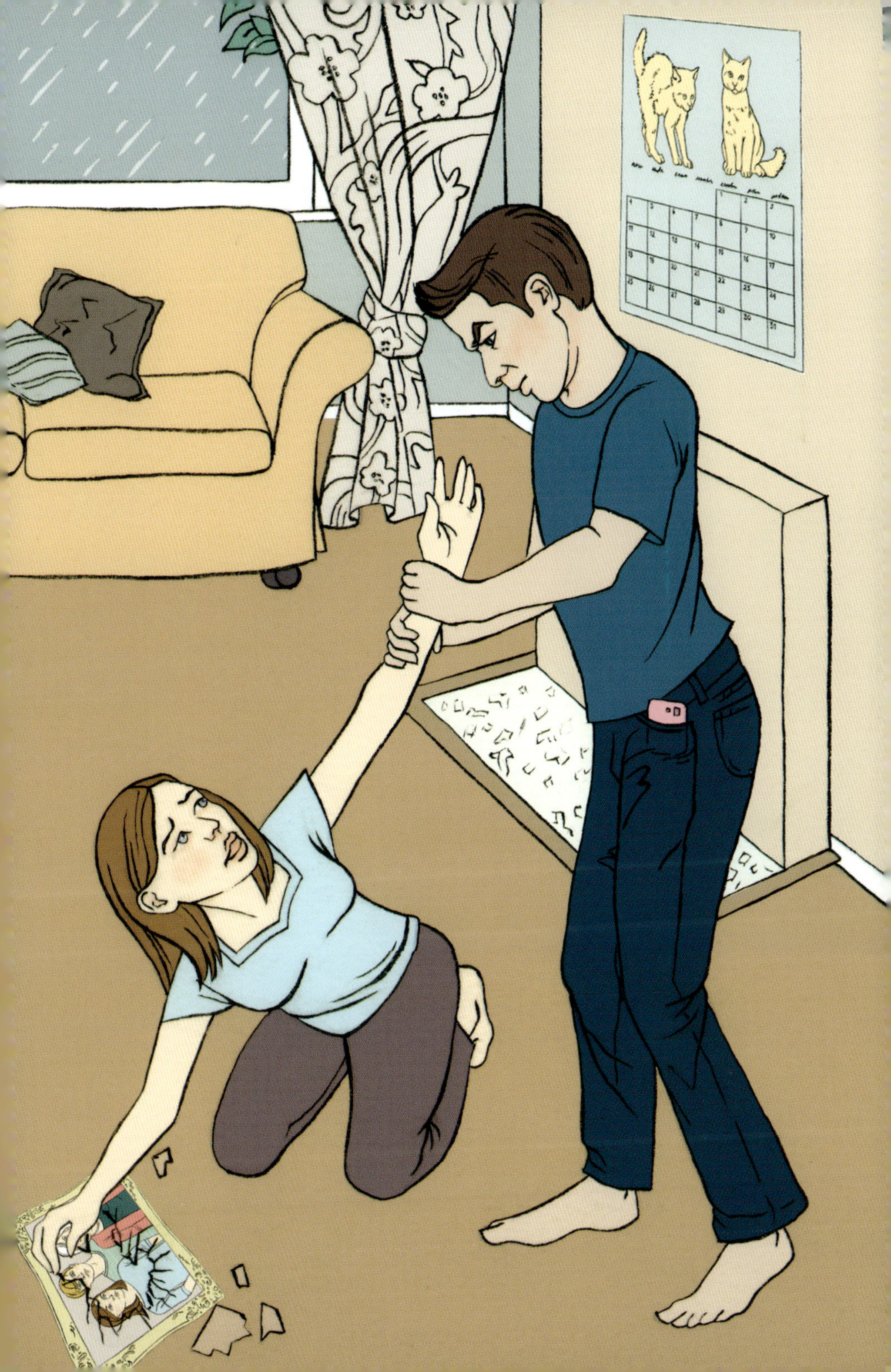

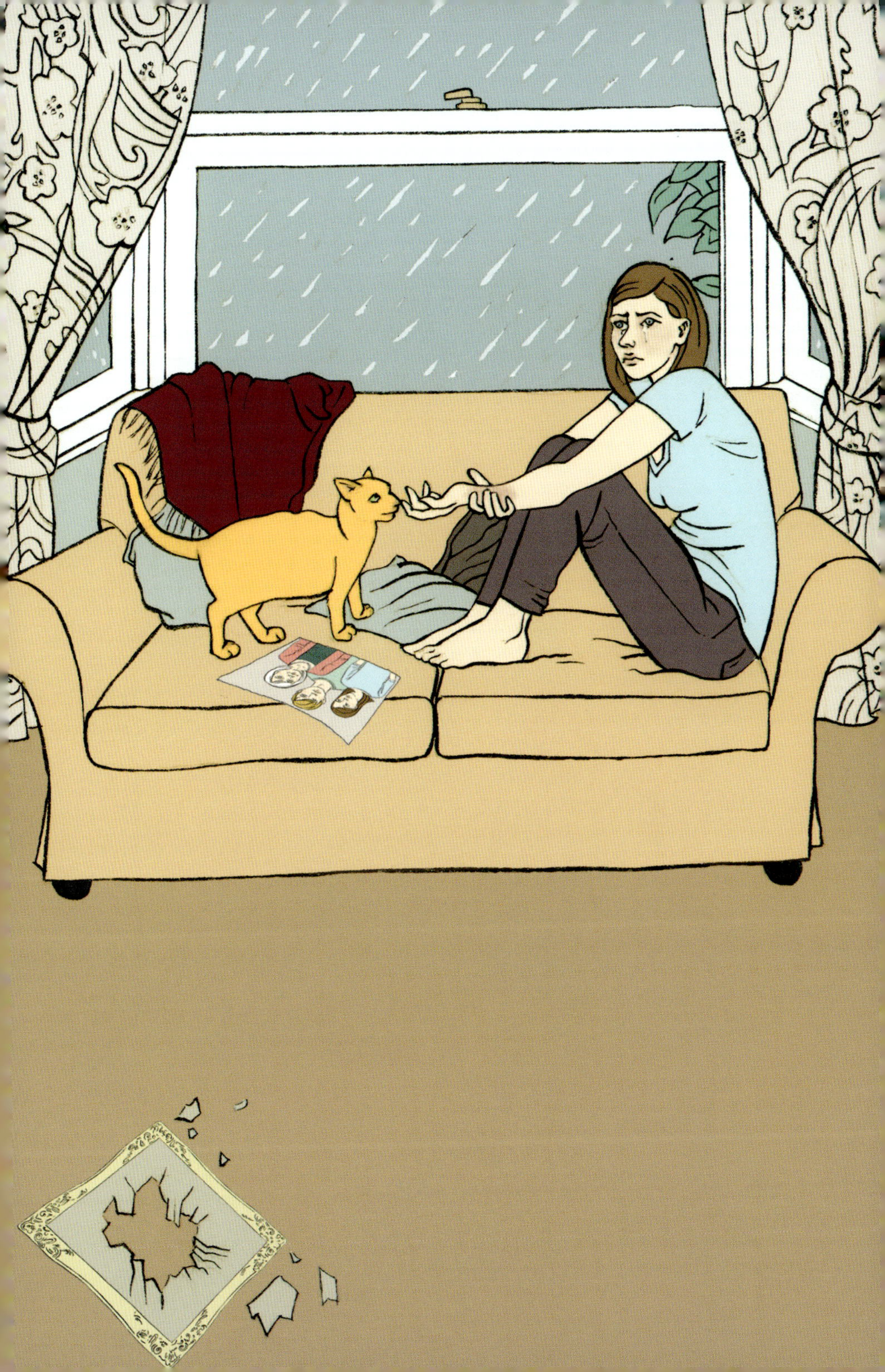

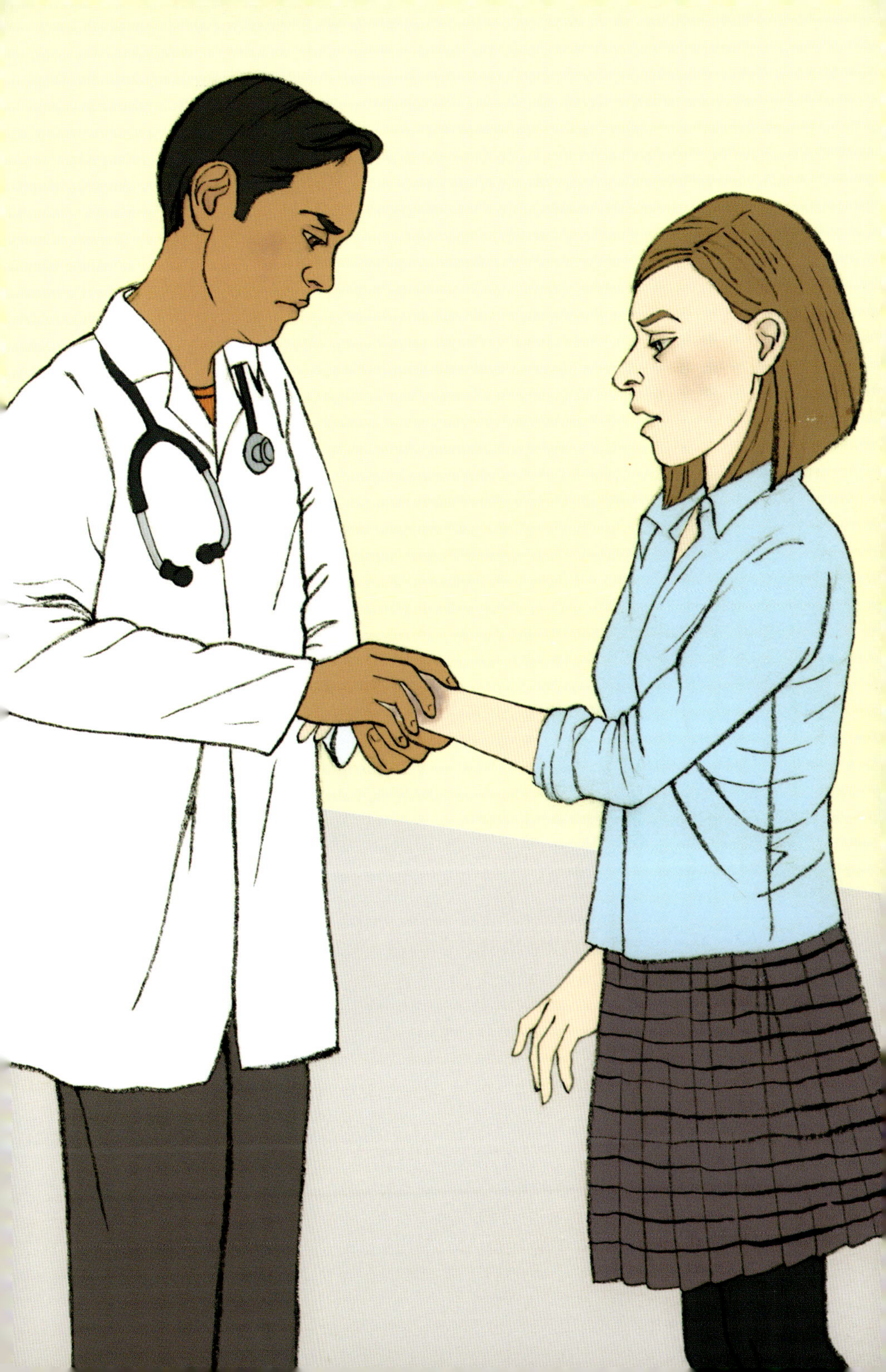

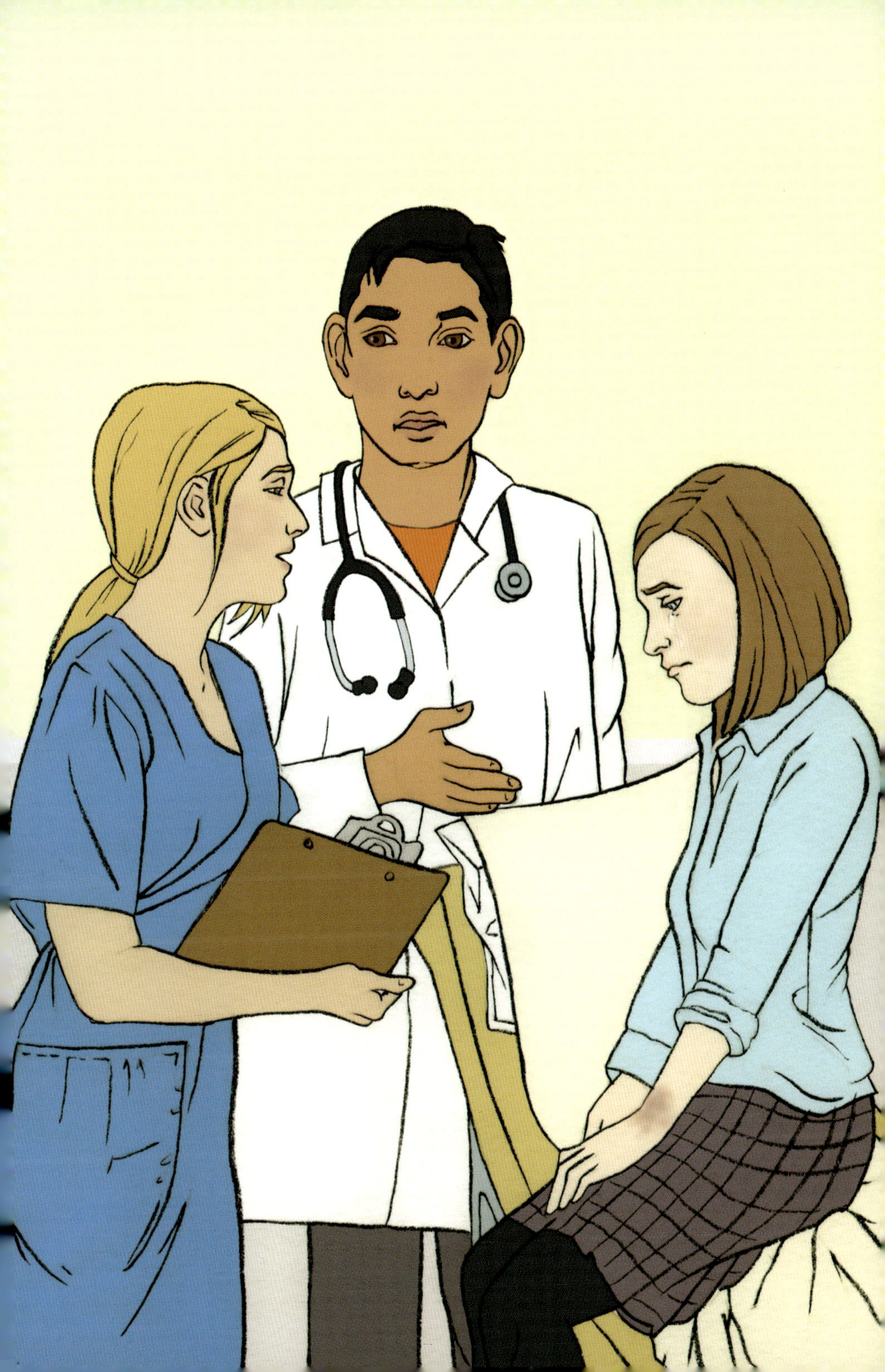

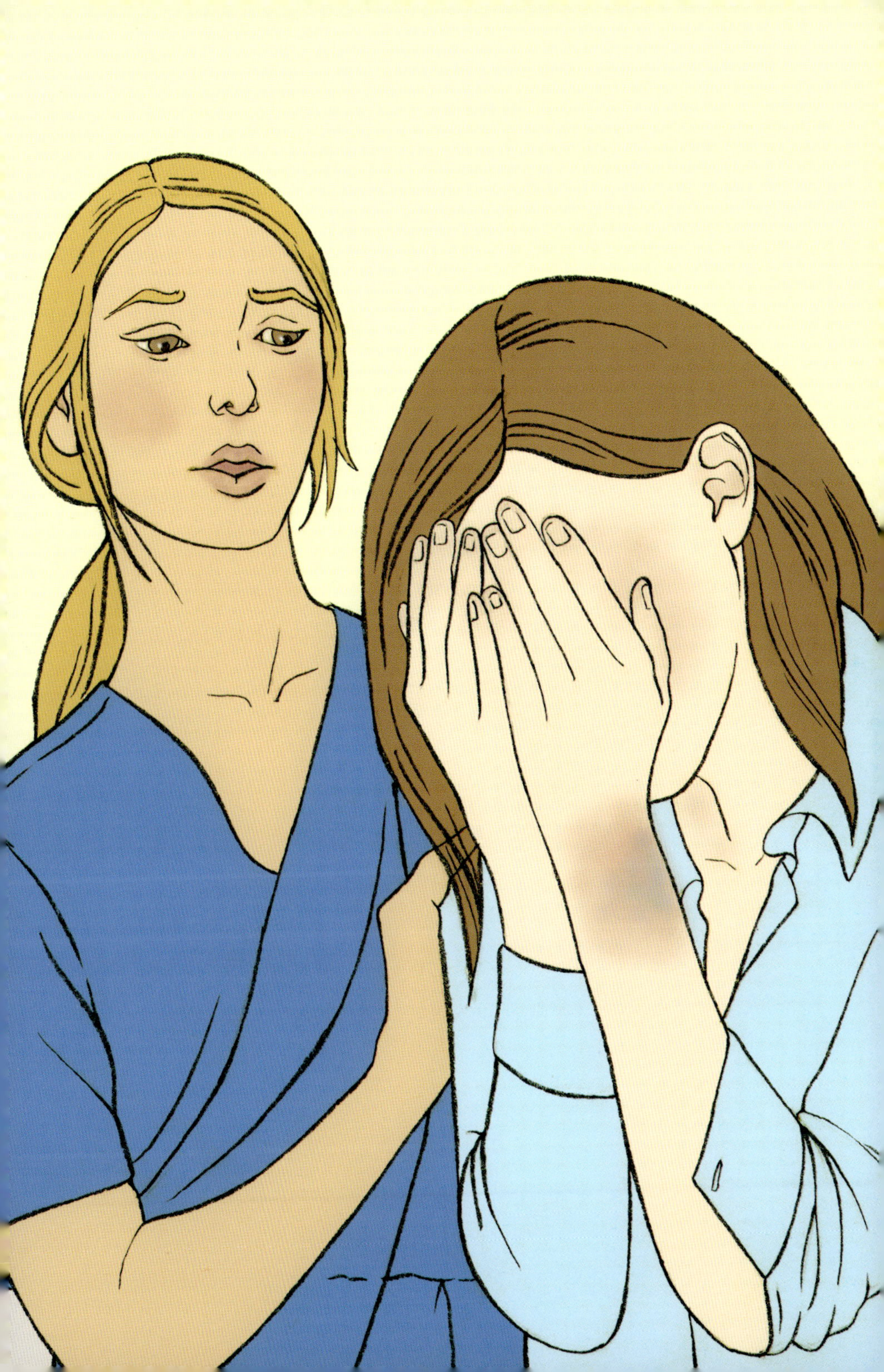

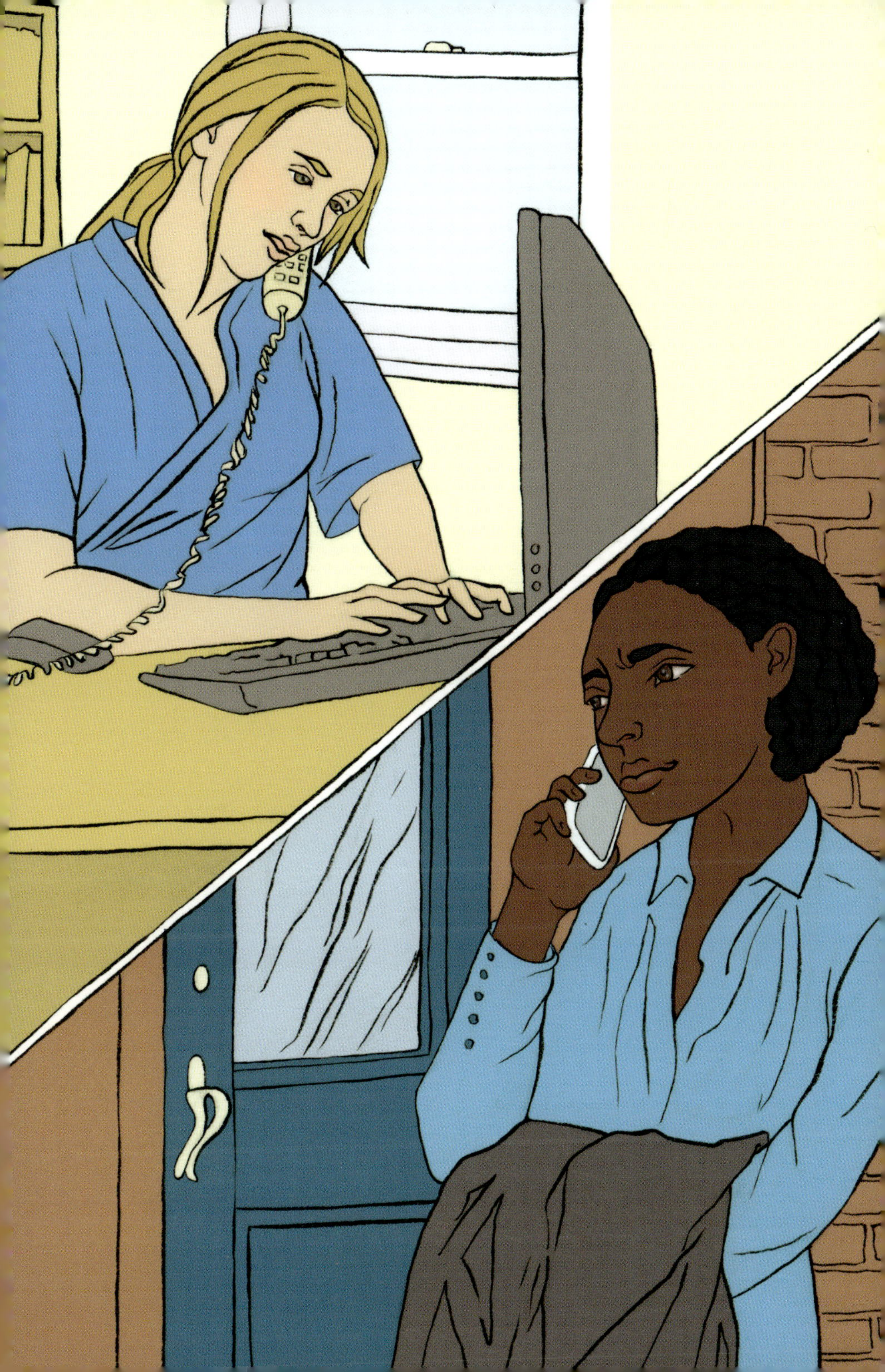

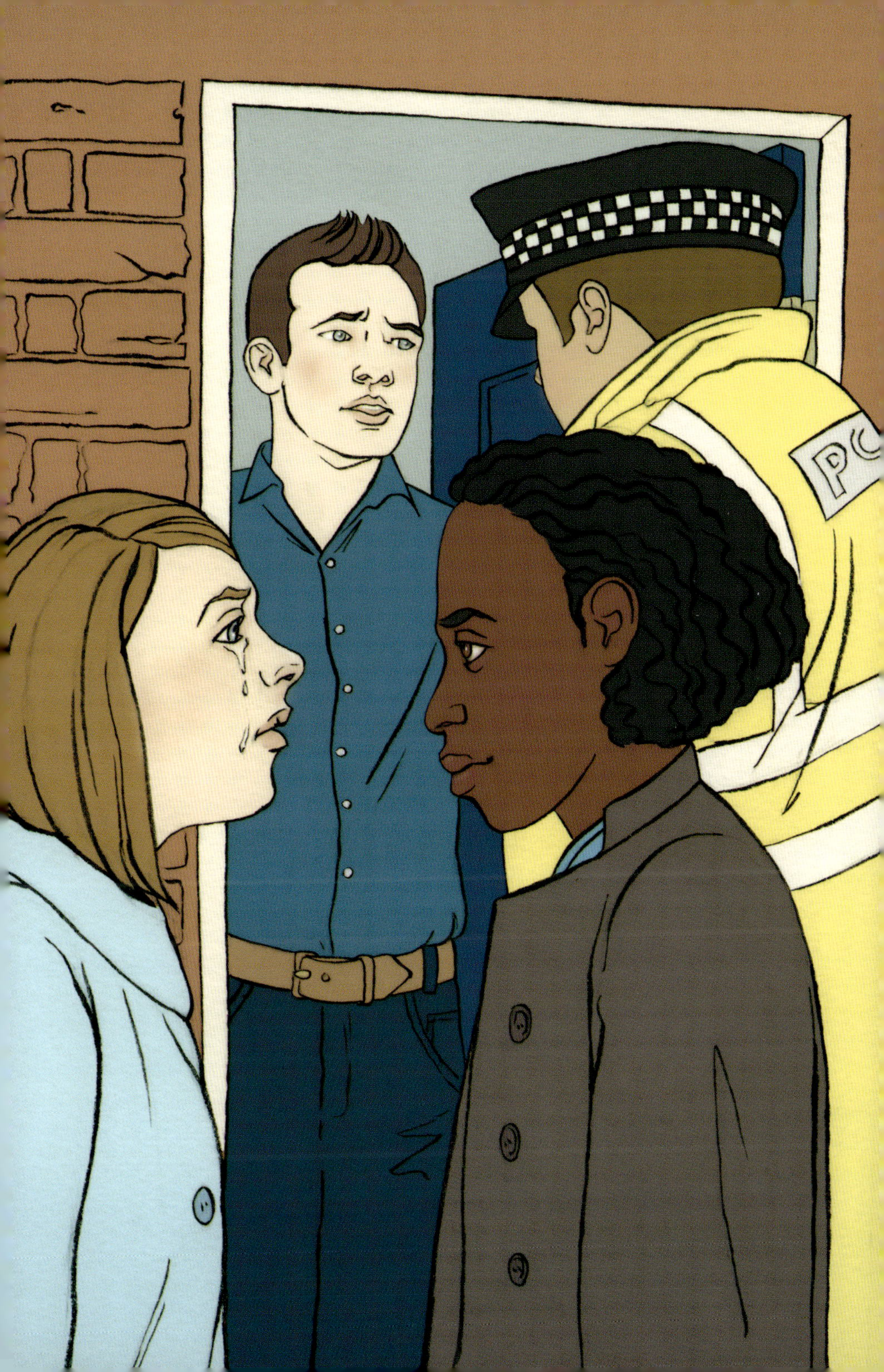

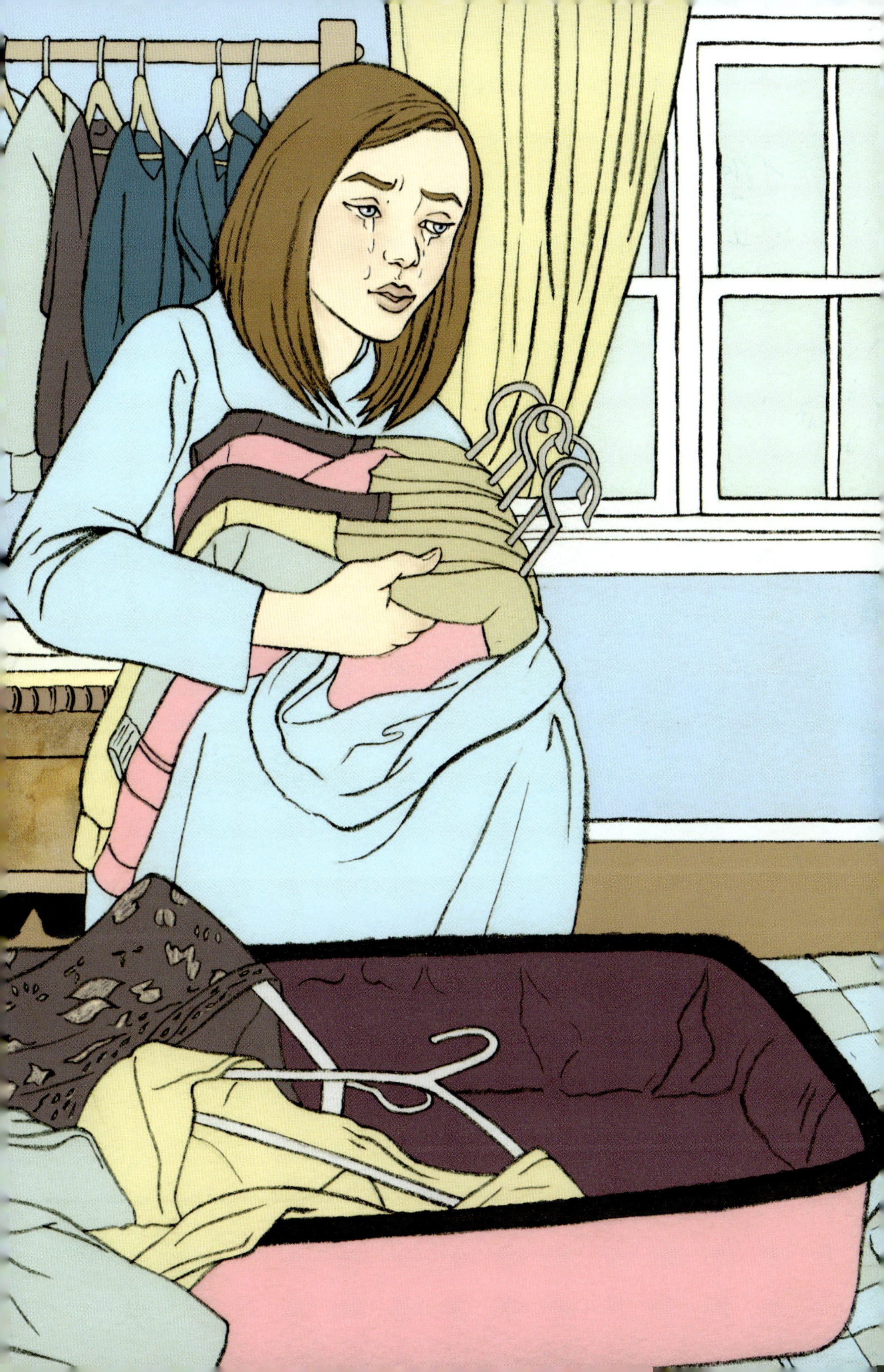

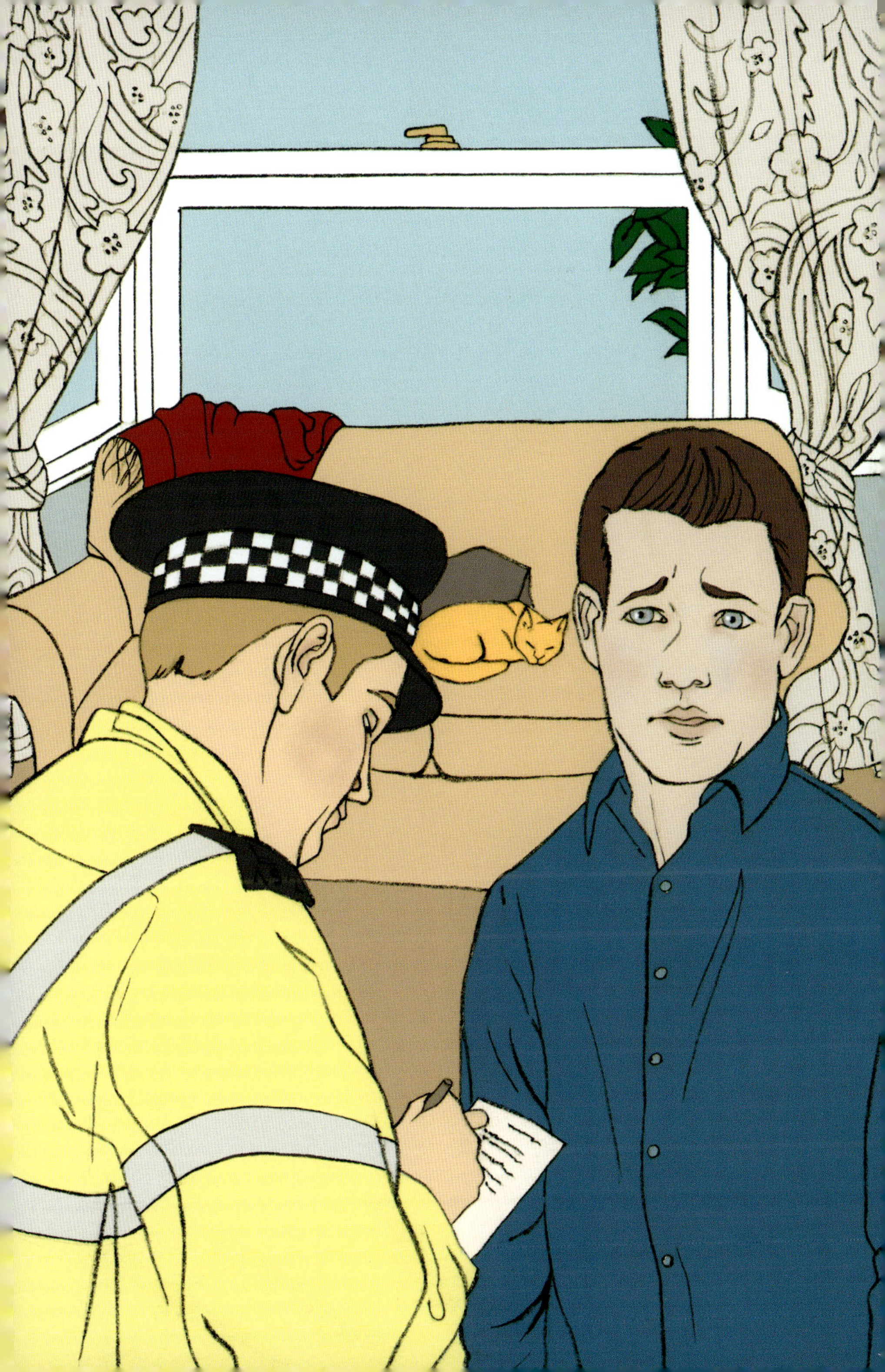

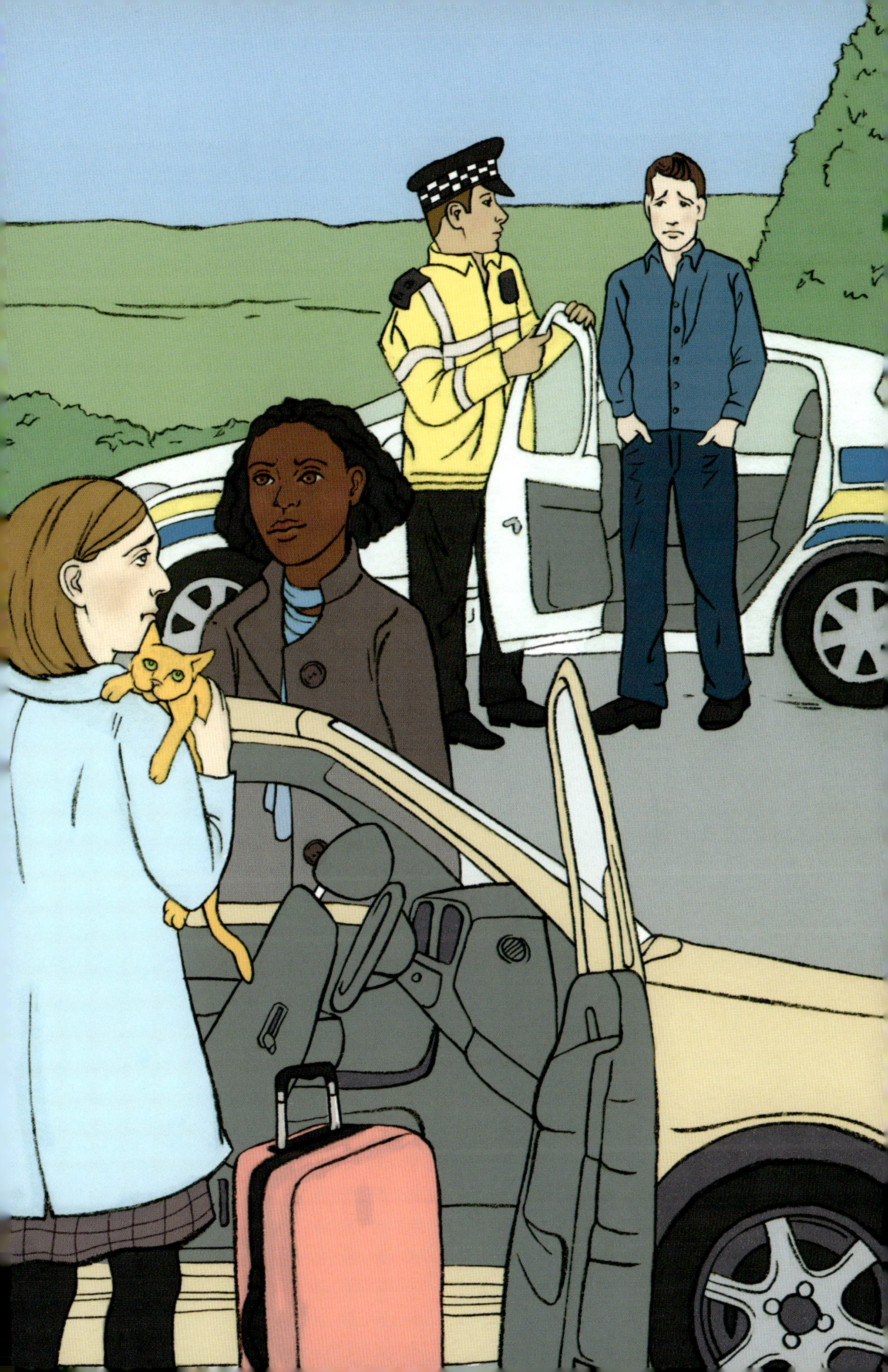

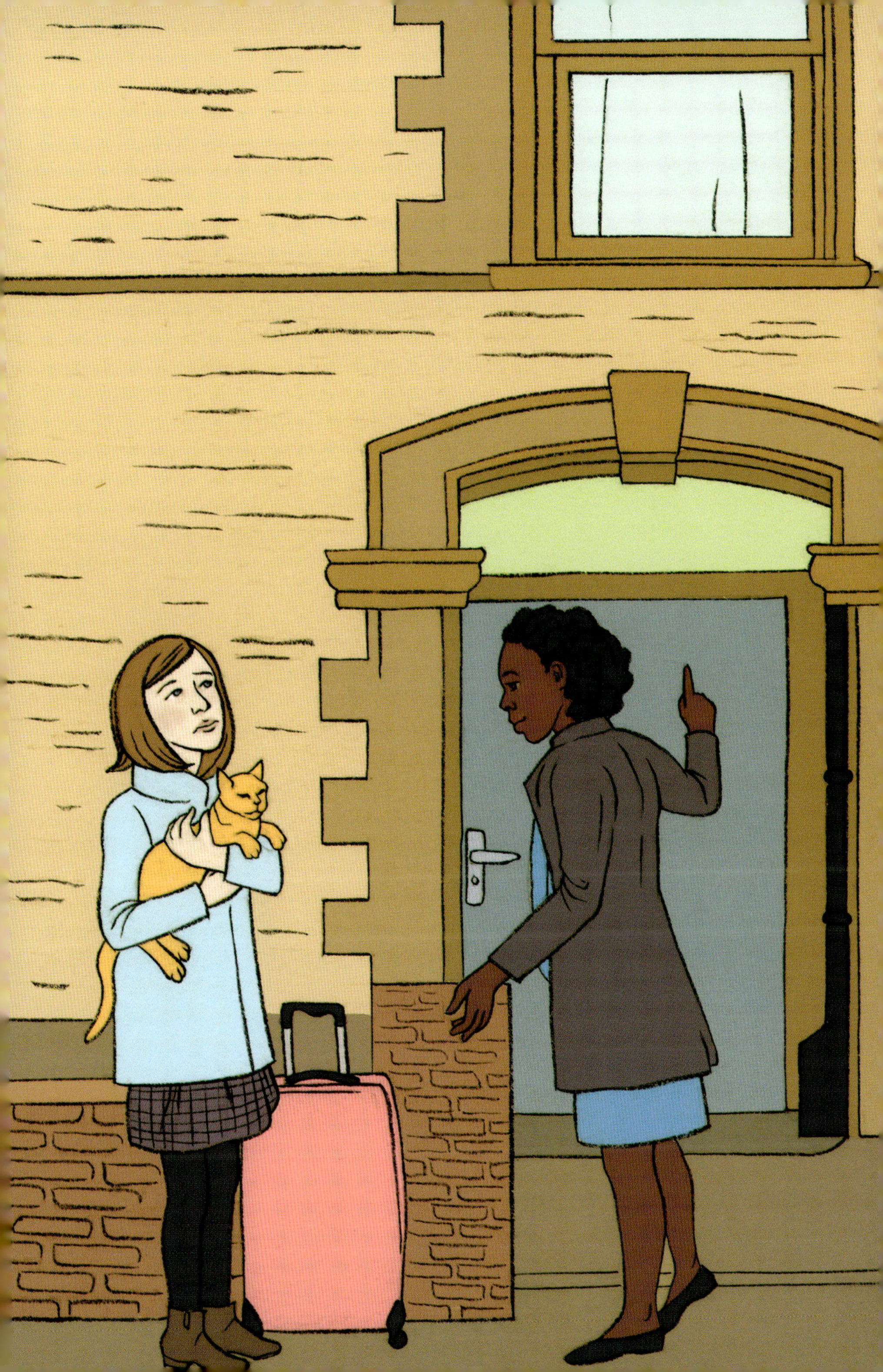

27

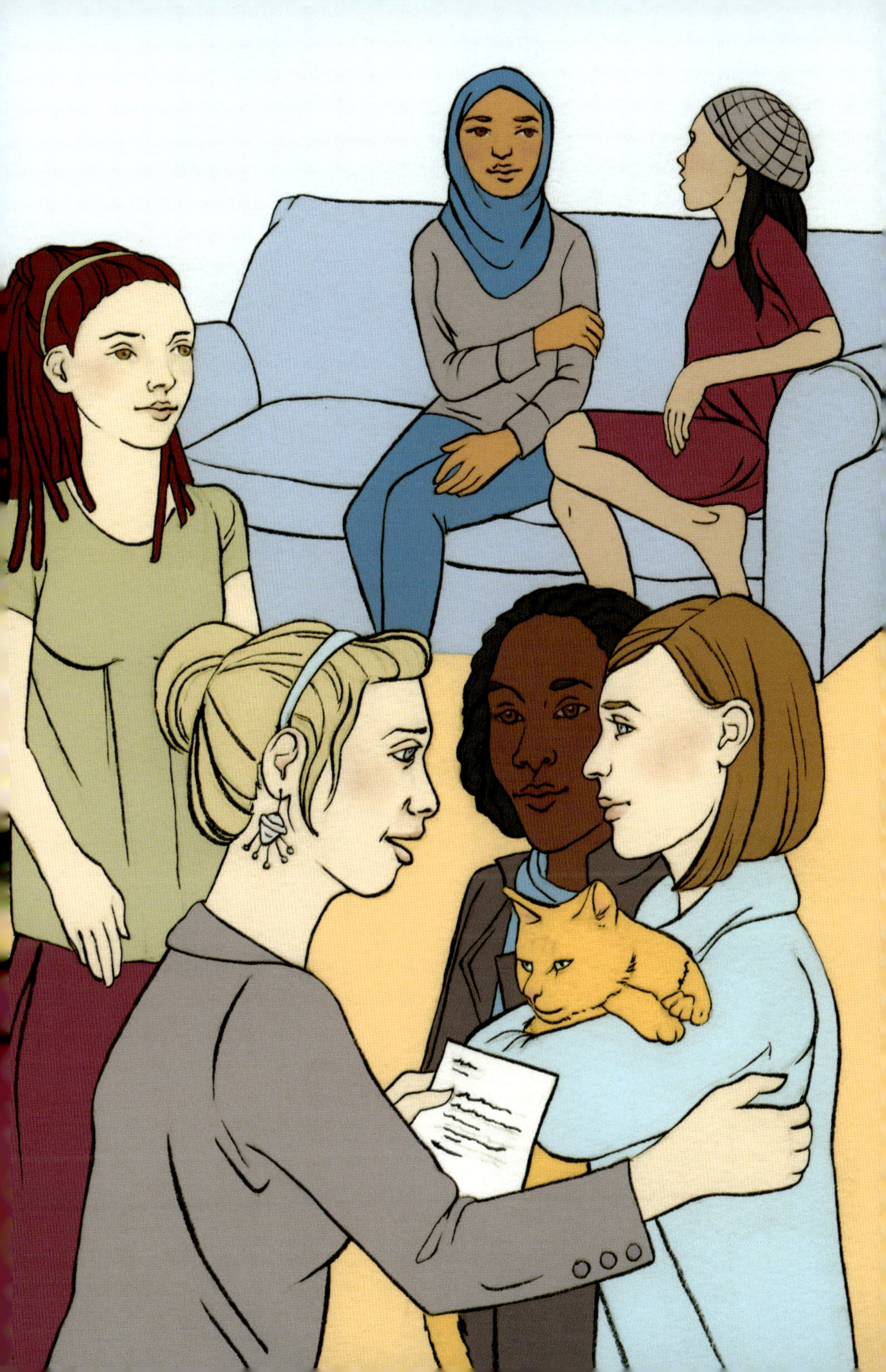

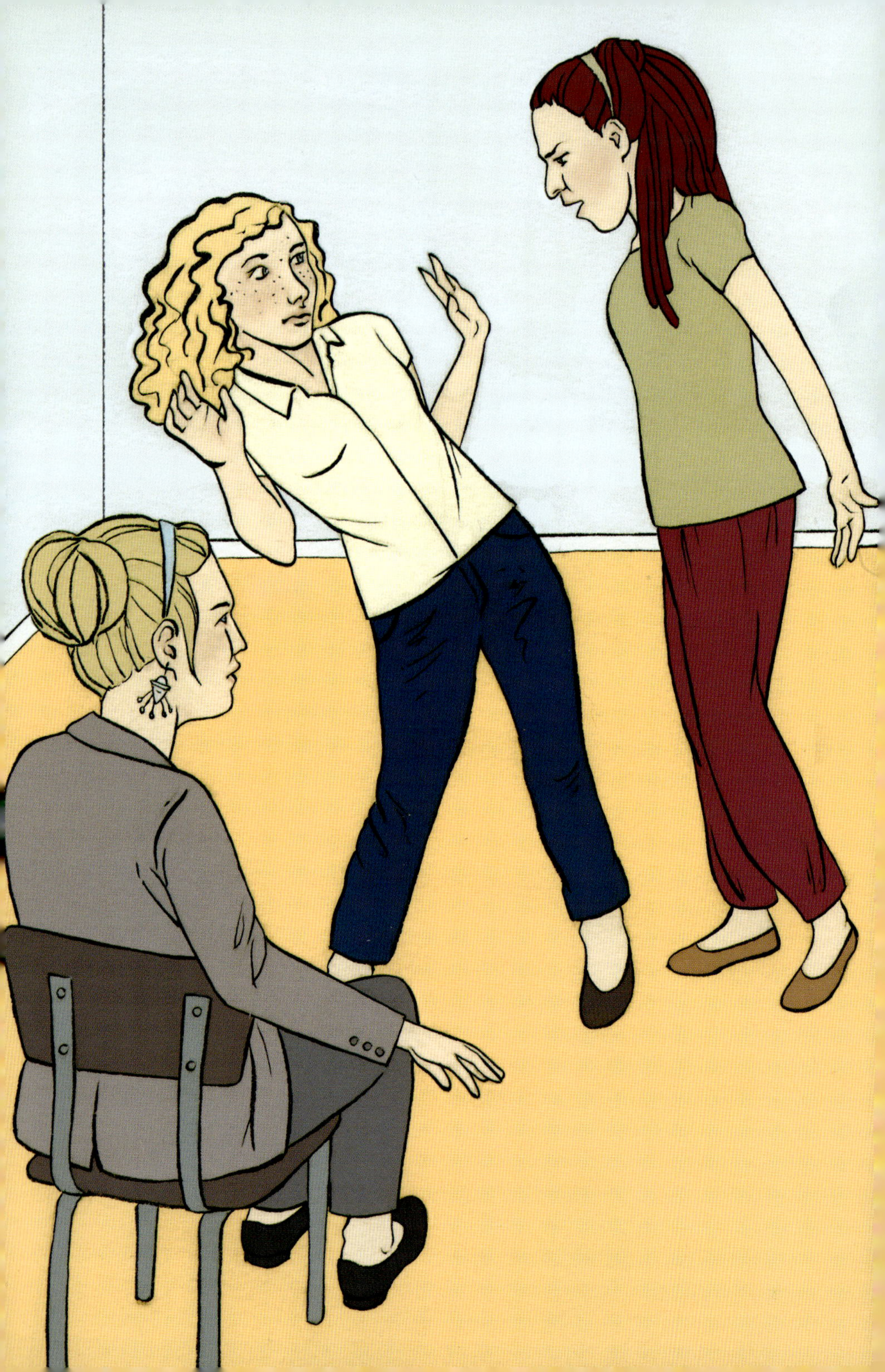

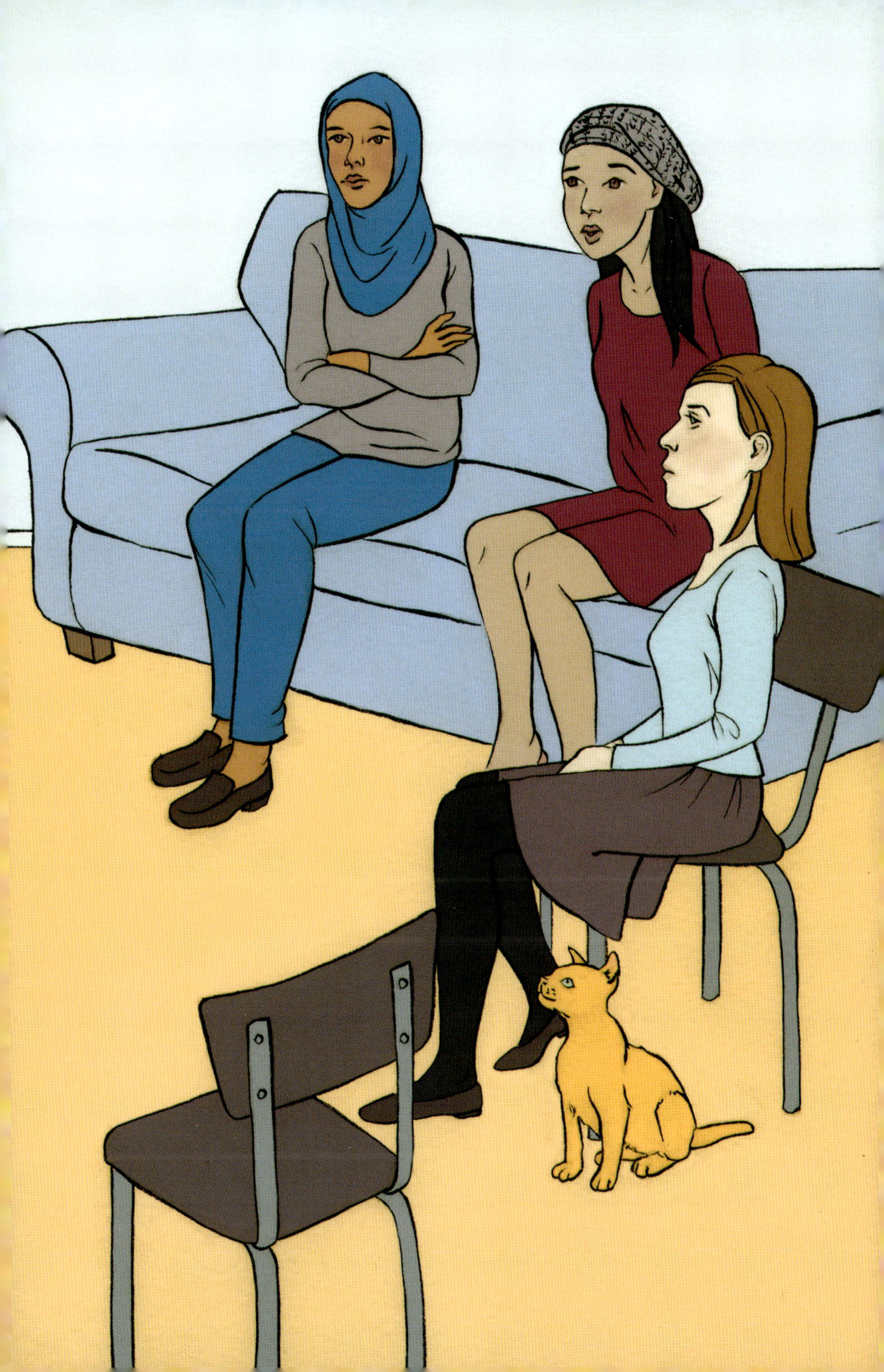

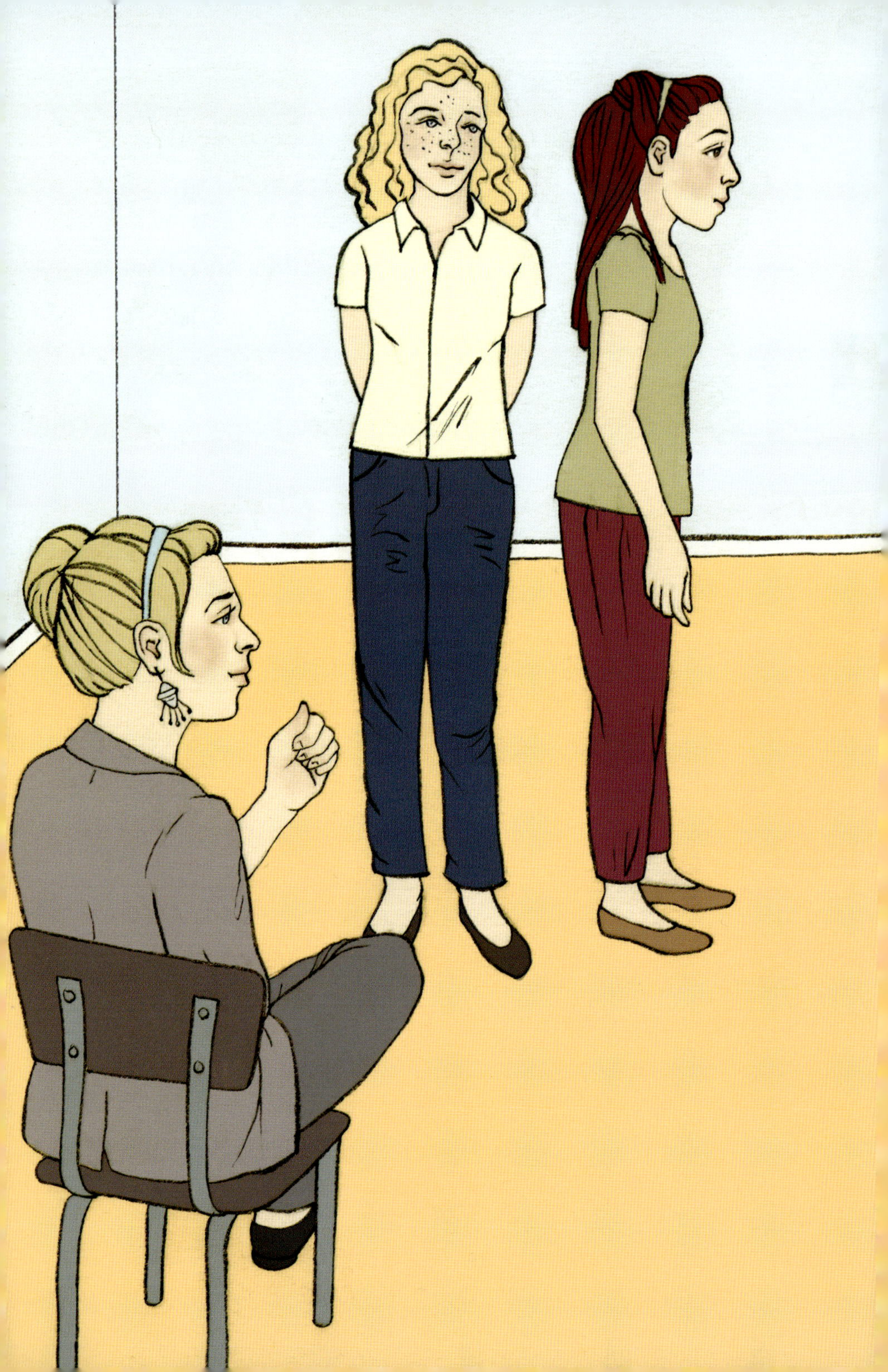

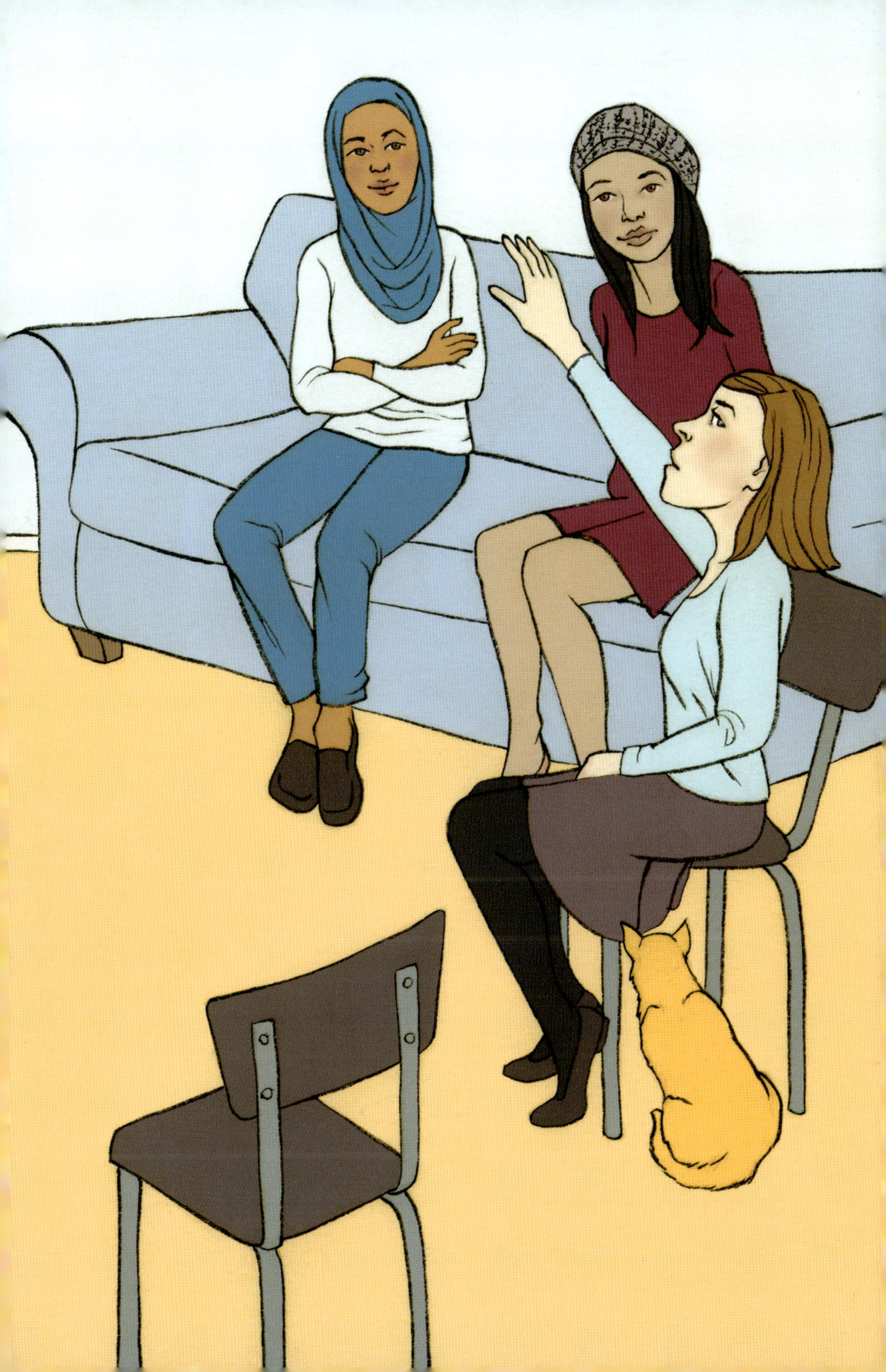

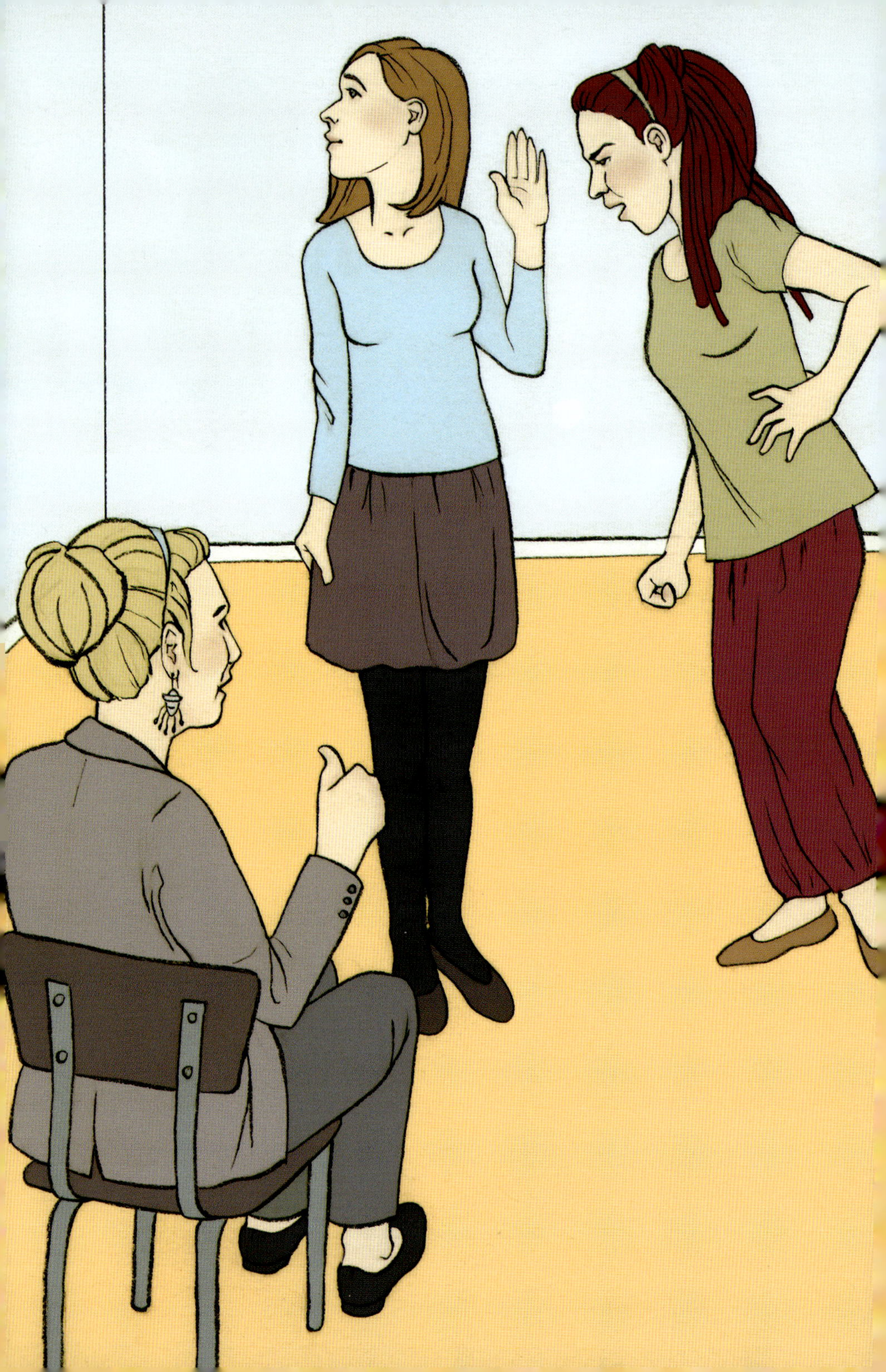

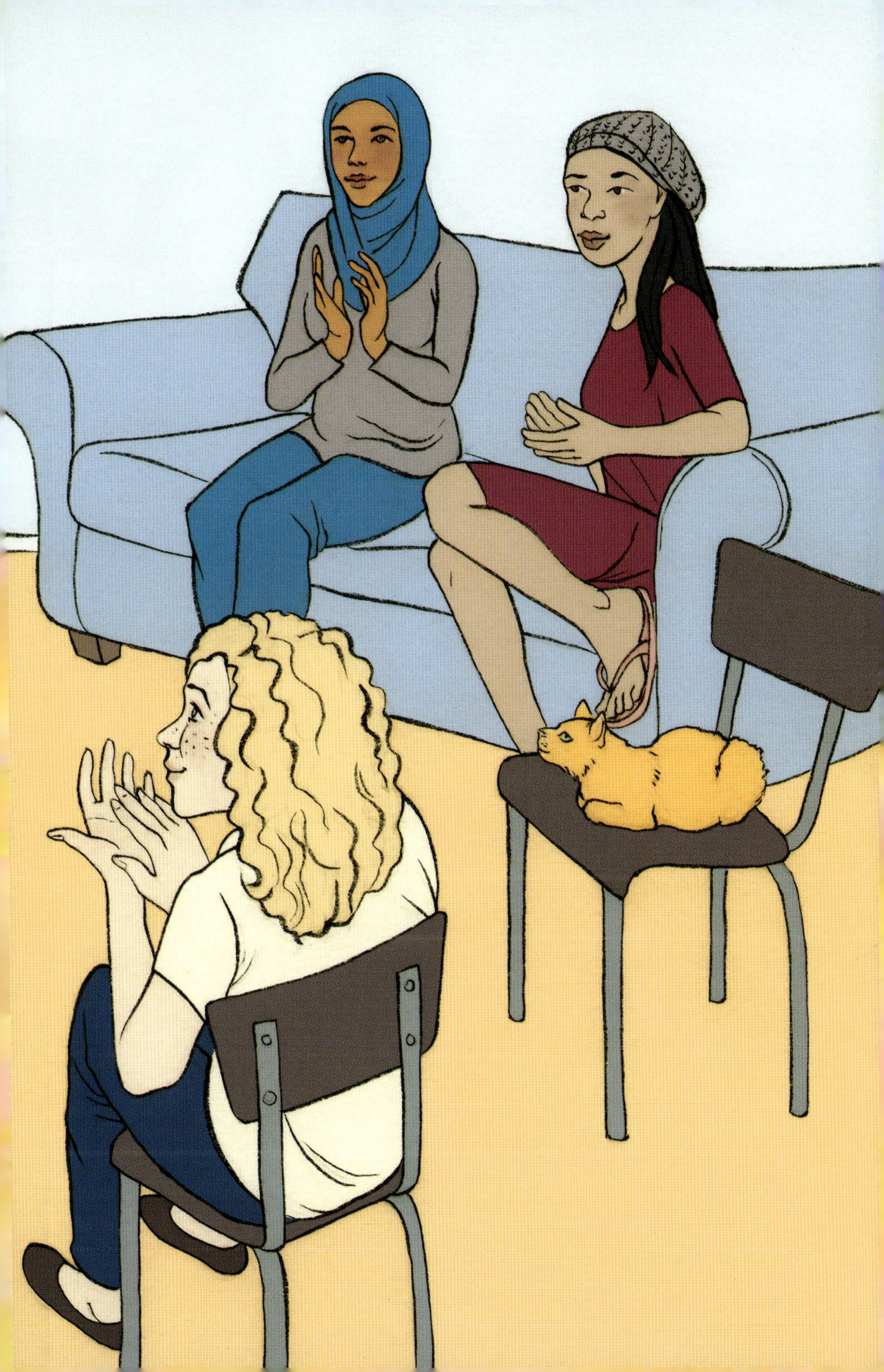

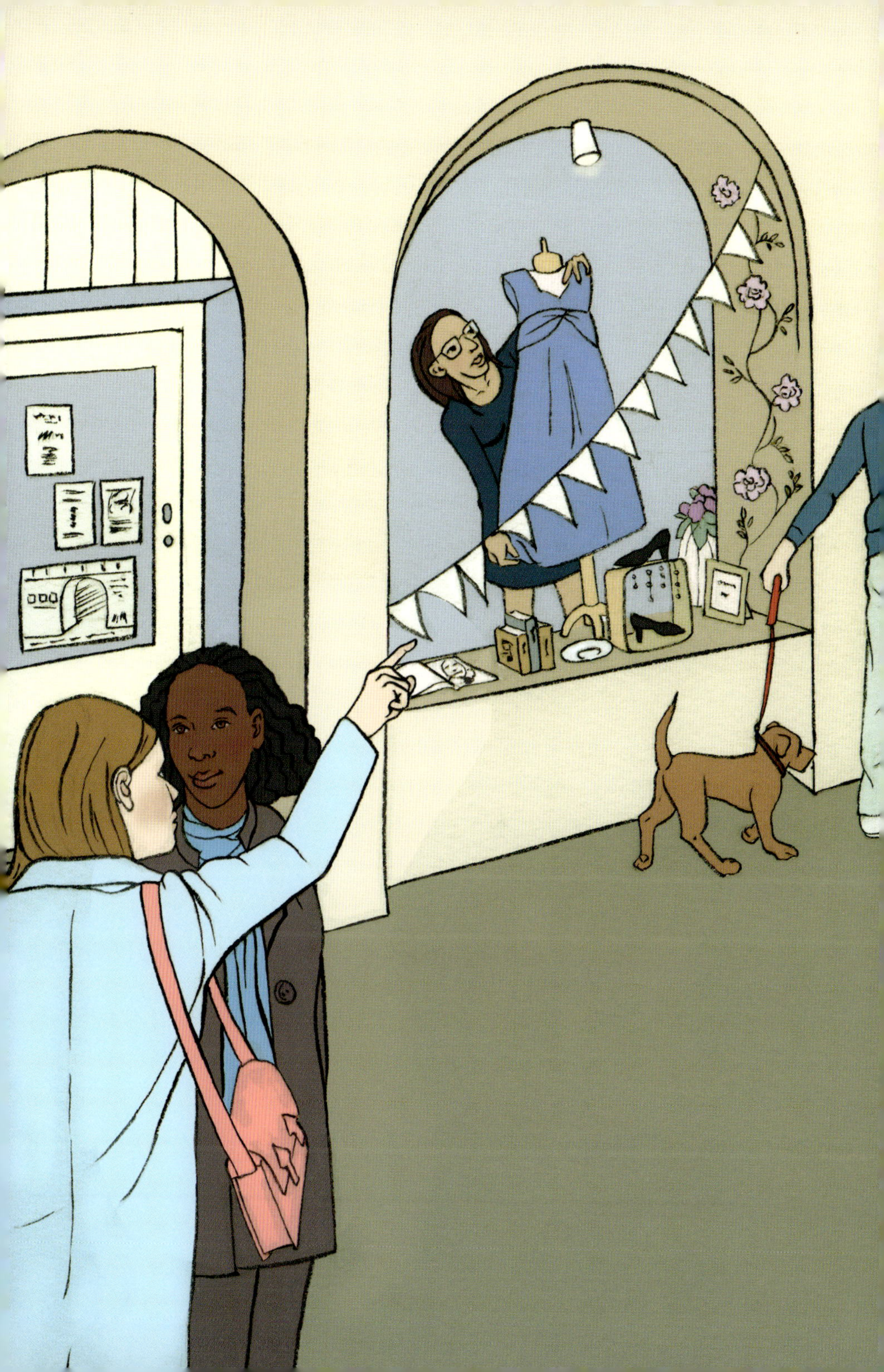

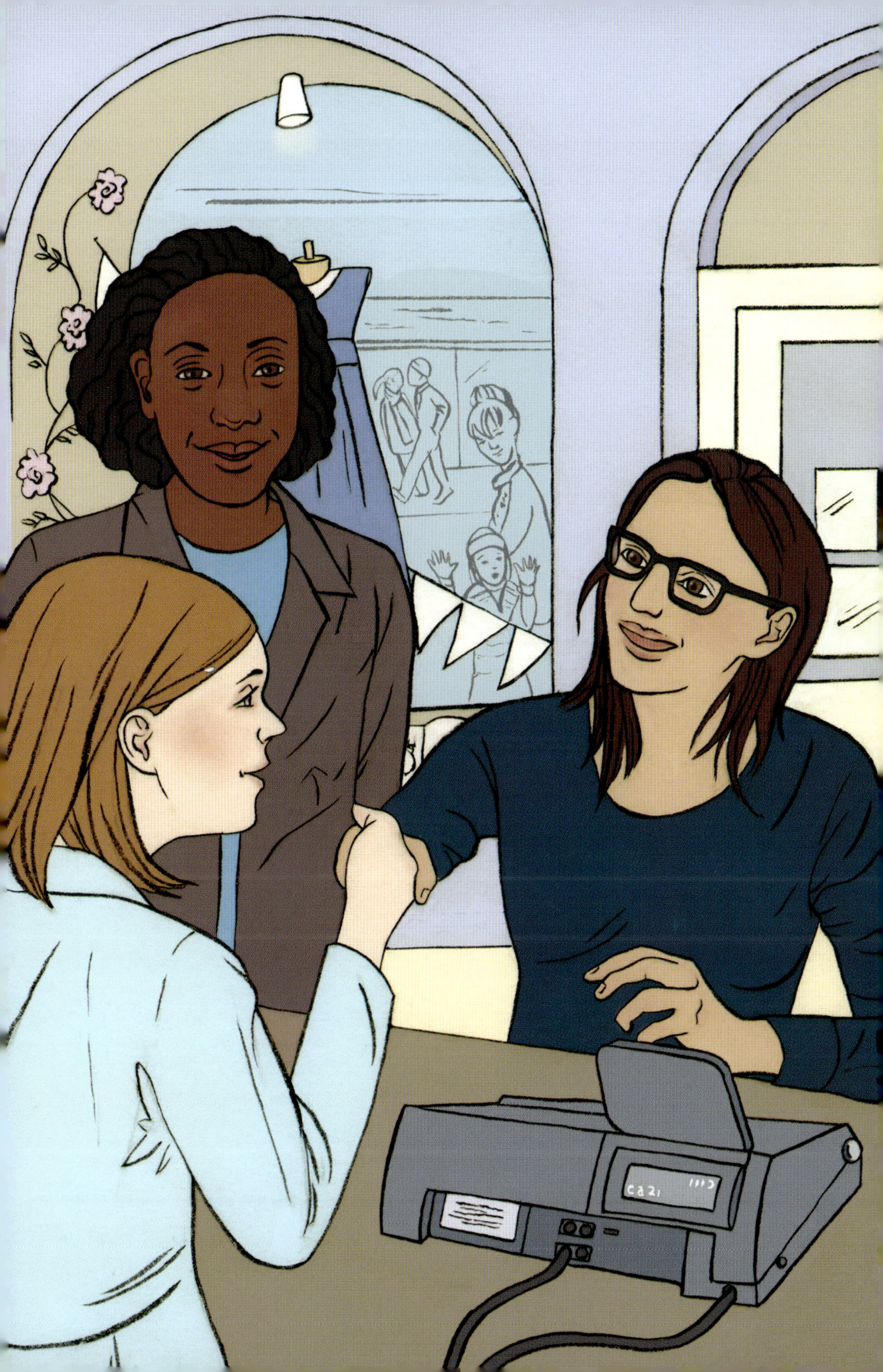

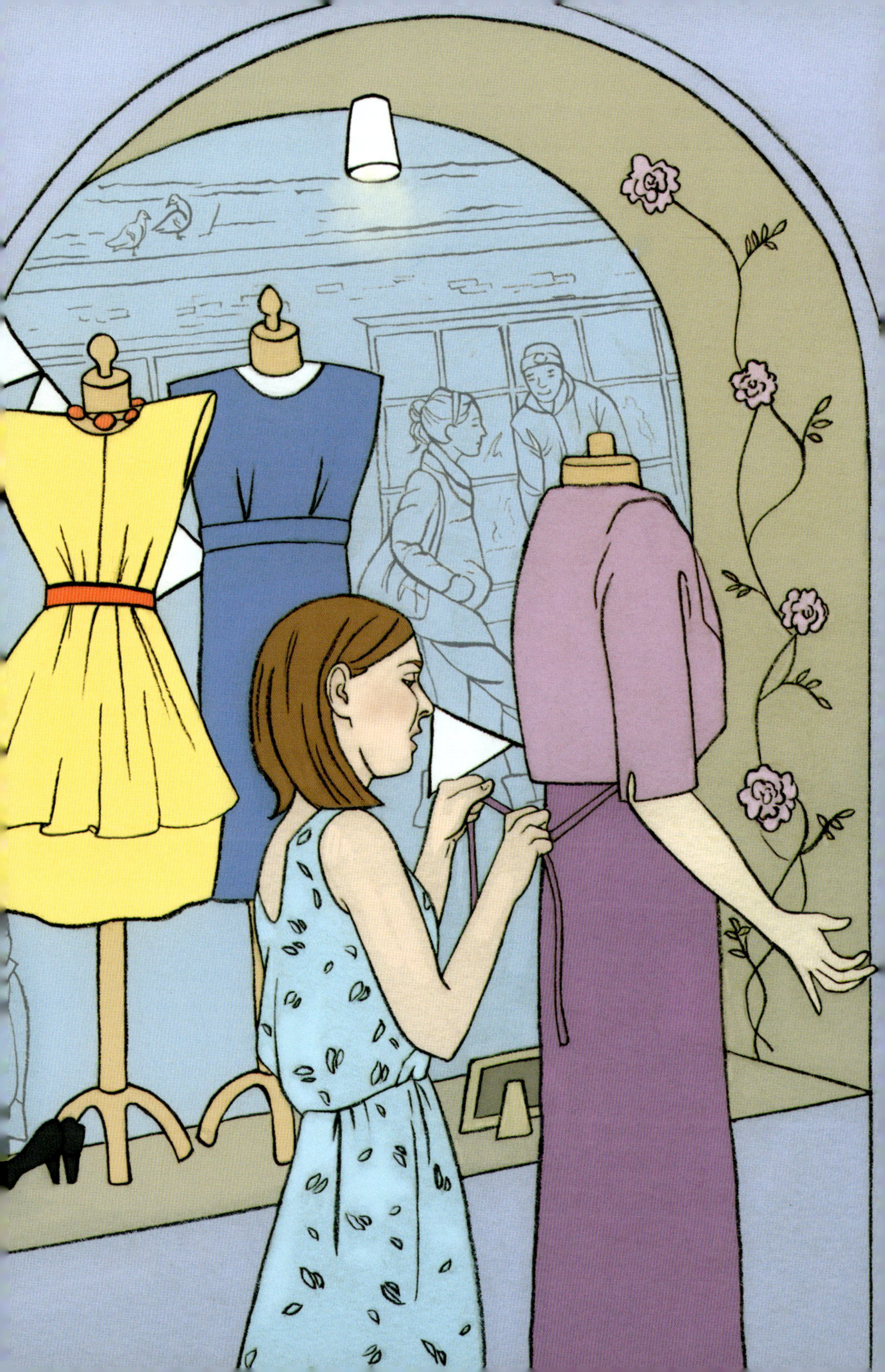

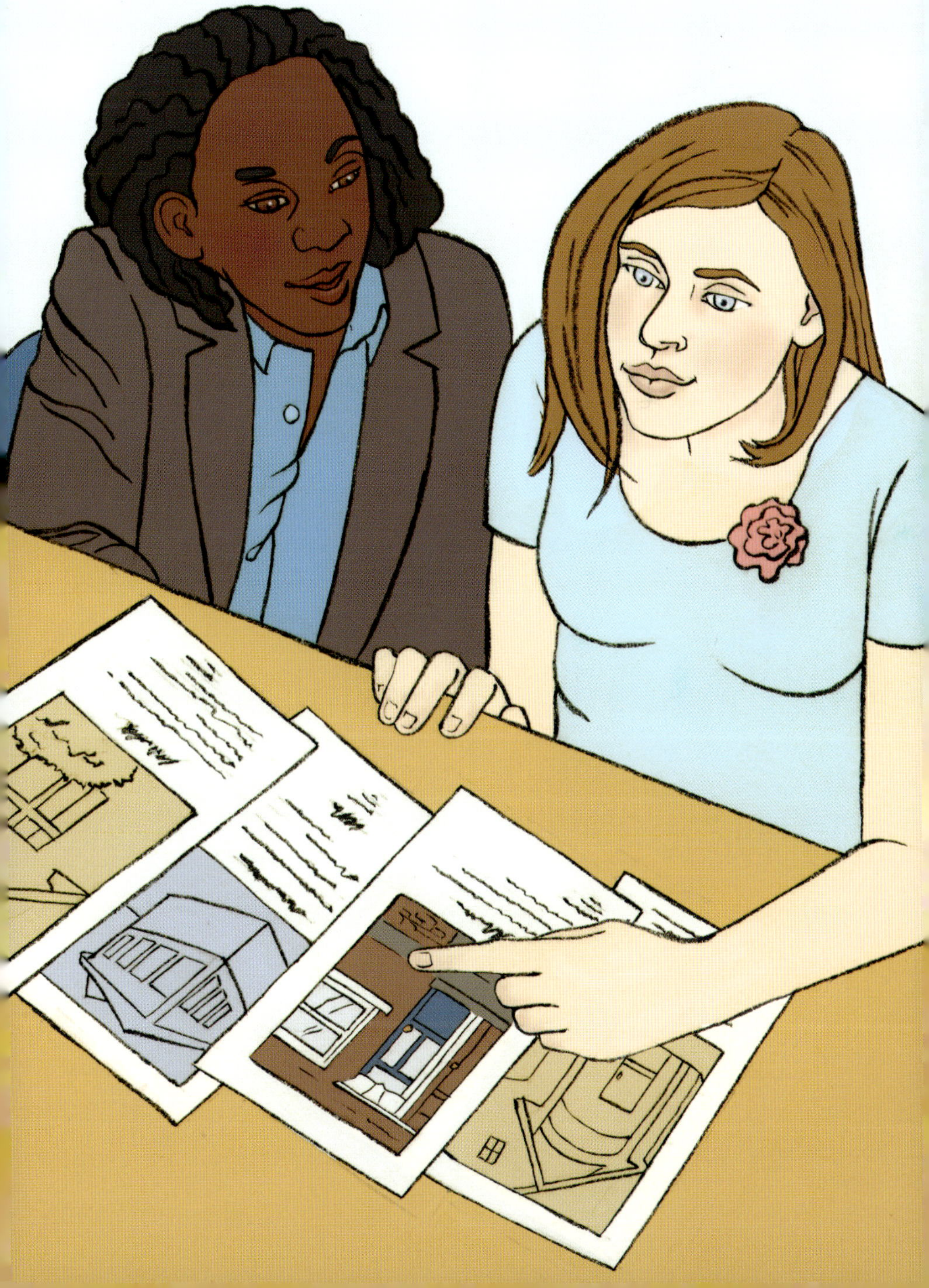

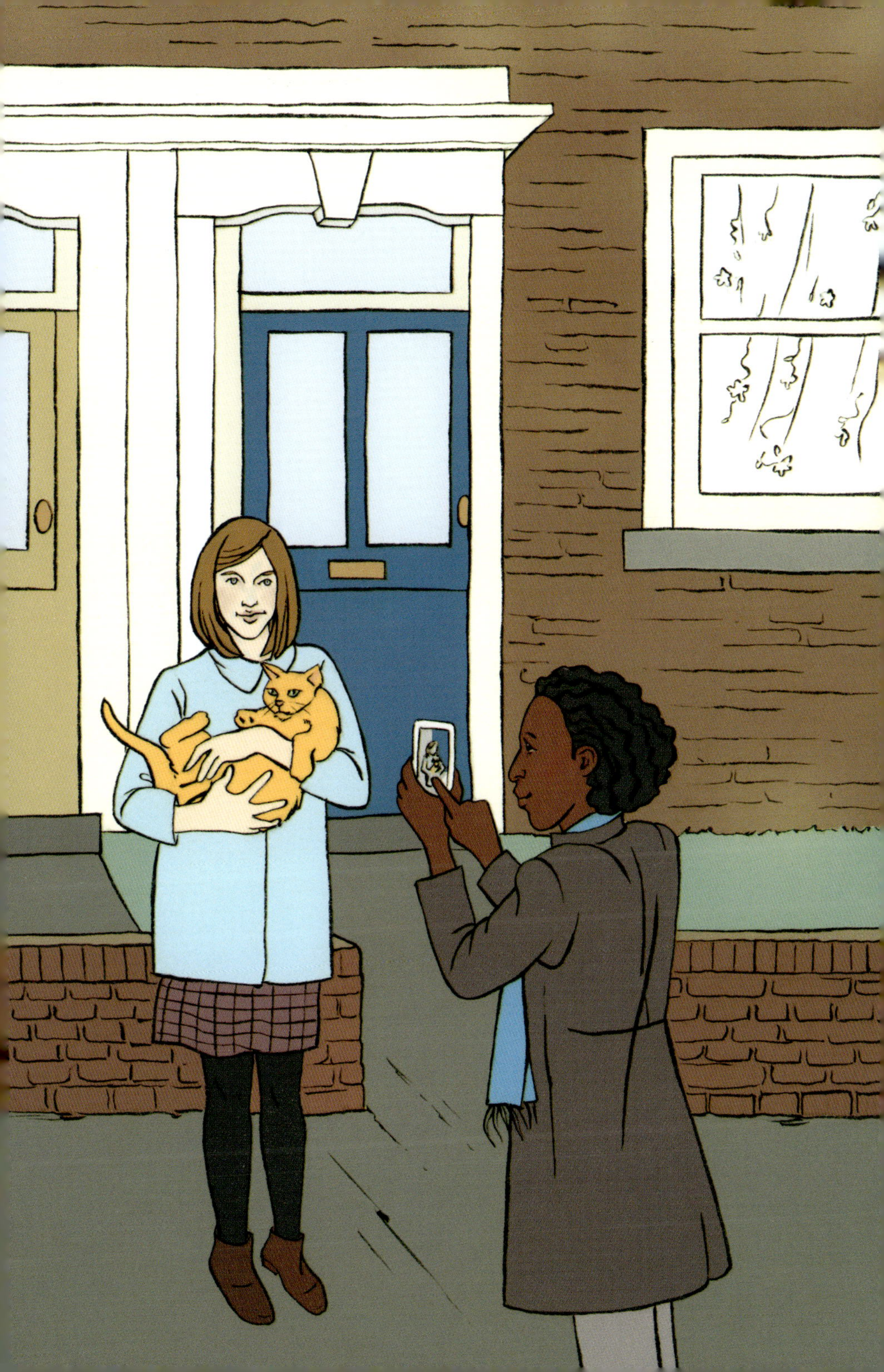

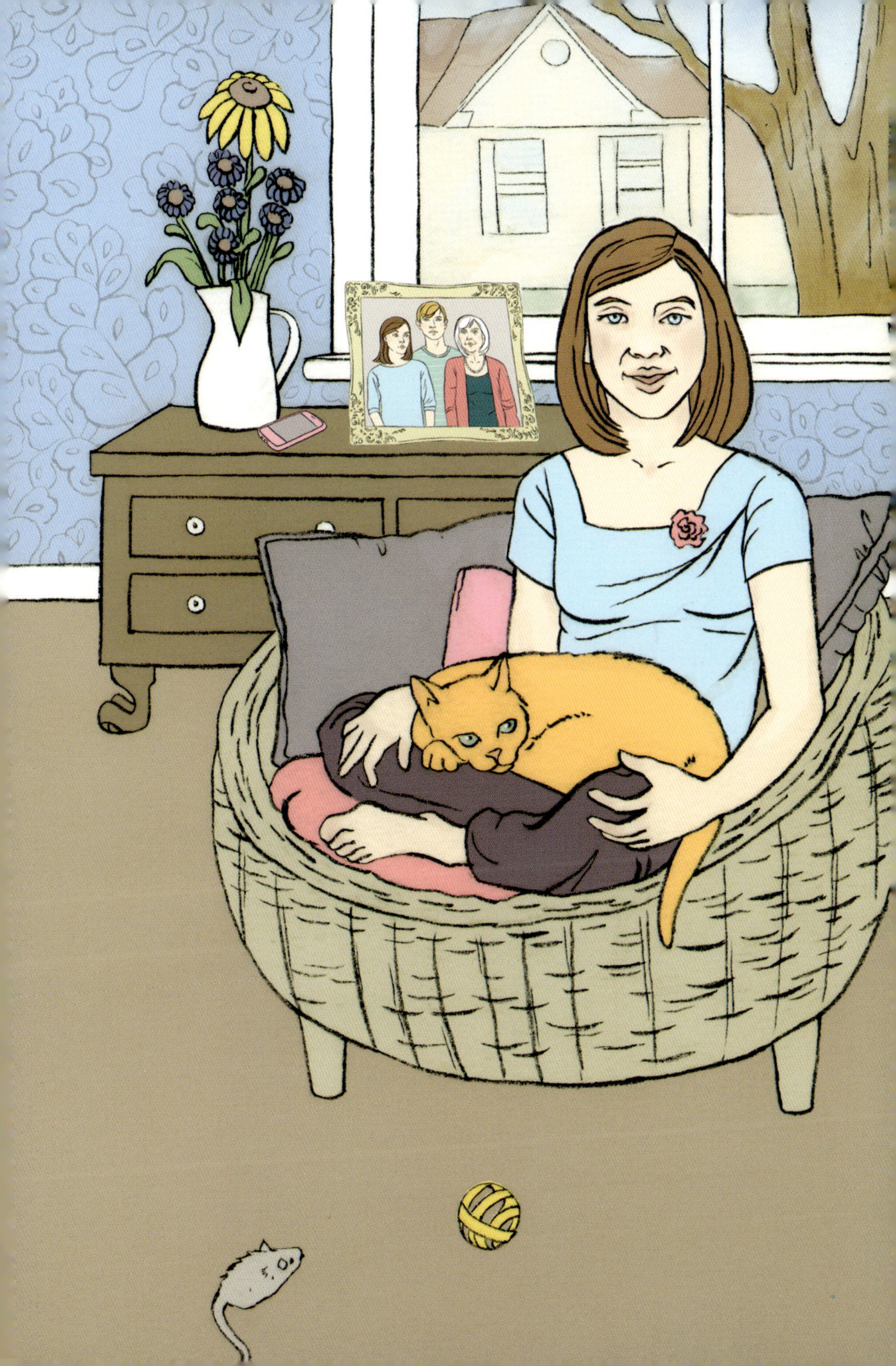

Storyline

The following words are provided for readers and supporters who want some ideas about one possible story. Most readers make their own story up from the pictures.

1. Katie and her friend Anne go to college. A boy sees Katie.
2. Katie and Anne enjoy their class. The teacher likes their work.
3. It's break time. Anne knows the boy. She introduces him to Katie. He is called David.
4. Katie and David go to the cinema. They sit close to each other.
5. It rains on the way home. Katie and David share an umbrella and hold hands. They are happy to be together.
6. Katie and David are with friends. They are a couple now.
7. Katie and David have dinner together. Katie is falling in love.
8. Katie moves into David's flat. Her cat Ginger comes too. David helps her unpack.
9. Katie puts a picture of her family on the mantlepiece.
10. Katie and David sit together on the sofa and relax. Katie has a cup of tea.

11. David asks Katie for money. He needs to pay for something.

12. David takes some more money from Katie's bag. He hasn't asked her, and she doesn't see him do it.

13. Katie is on the phone to her family. She tells them about her new home. David watches her. He is jealous.

14. Now David shouts at Katie. He takes her phone. Katie is frightened. She doesn't understand. "Why are you cross with me?"

15. David throws the picture of Katie's family on the floor and it smashes. He is really angry. Katie feels shocked and sad.

16. Katie picks up the picture. But David grabs her arm and hurts her wrist.

17. David has gone out. Katie sits on the sofa with Ginger. She is very upset about what happened. Her wrist is sore.

18. Katie goes to the doctor about her sore wrist. The doctor looks at it. Katie is quiet. She doesn't want to say what happened.

19. The doctor brings in a nurse to help. Maybe Katie will talk to the nurse.

20. Katie thinks about what happened and starts crying. The nurse comforts her. She can help.

21. The nurse calls another woman who can help. Her name is Brenda.

22. Brenda goes with Katie to the flat. The police are there too. David opens the door. He is surprised and worried.

23. Katie packs up her clothes. She still feels very upset about what happened. She is going to go somewhere safe.

24. The police officer asks David what happened.

25. Katie and Ginger go in the car with Brenda. The police officer takes David to the police station to answer more questions.

26. Katie, Brenda and Ginger are at a safe house.

27. The other people at the safe house welcome Katie. There are only women here. Katie can stay and be safe.

28. Some of the women at the safe house are doing a role play. One woman is pretending to shout, and another one is pretending to be frightened.

29. The play has stopped. Katie puts her hand up. She has an idea about what to do.

30. The play starts again. The woman is still pretending to shout, but Katie puts her hand up. "No! You can't shout at me," she says. The other women clap.

31. Katie and Brenda are in town. Katie sees a shop she likes. "Maybe I could get a job there," she says.

32. Katie and Brenda go to the shop together. The woman in the shop is telling Katie about a job.

33. Now Katie works in the shop. She likes her new job.

34. Katie and Brenda look at some pictures of places to live. Katie chooses a picture of a house she likes. She can live there soon.

35. Brenda, Katie and Ginger arrive at the house. Brenda takes a picture of Katie outside her new home.

36. Katie is in her new home. She has Ginger with her. Her picture is mended too. She is safe and happy.

What is domestic abuse?

Domestic abuse is the name given to abuse between people who are in, or have been in, an intimate or family-type relationship. It's not the victim's fault.

Domestic abuse is when one person in a relationship tries to dominate and control the other person through threats, violence or other abuse. It can take the form of physical, psychological, sexual or financial abuse, and a pattern of bullying and controlling behaviour develops. This can include forced marriage and so-called 'honour' crimes. Domestic abuse that includes physical violence is sometimes called domestic violence.

Domestic abuse is very common and can happen in both heterosexual and same-sex partnerships. It can happen to people of all ages, ethnic backgrounds, and economic levels. And while women are more commonly victims of domestic abuse, it can happen to men, too.

Growing up in a family where there is domestic abuse can leave a young person with painful and overwhelming emotions of guilt, betrayal and rejection. It can have a considerable impact on how they grow up and form their own relationships. Sometimes people who have grown up in a home where there is domestic abuse later enter into intimate relationships which become abusive. This may be because some of the behaviour that is abusive has come to seem normal to them. Domestic abuse can have a long-lasting and damaging effect on everyone involved.

What is not safe in a relationship?

Abusive behaviour is never acceptable, whether by a man, a woman, a teenager, or an older adult.

The abuse can take the form of emotional abuse, which could include verbal abuse such as yelling, name-calling, blaming, and shaming. It can also be controlling behaviour, such as isolating the person or frightening them with threats. The abuse can escalate from threats and verbal abuse to violence. And while physical injury may seem the most obvious danger, the emotional and psychological consequences of domestic abuse are serious and long-lasting. Emotionally abusive relationships can destroy a person's self-worth, and can lead to anxiety and depression, making the person feel helpless and alone.

Below is a list of the kinds of behaviour that would be considered to be domestic abuse:

- disrespect: regular criticism; persistently putting the person down in front of other people or embarrassing them in public; not listening or responding when they talk; interrupting telephone calls

- verbal abuse: shouting; mocking; accusing; name-calling; verbally threatening

- use of pressure tactics: sulking; threatening or attempting suicide; threatening to make reports to agencies unless the person gives in to the abuser's demands

- removing choice and power: telling the other person that they have no choice in any decisions;

lying or withholding information; withholding or pressuring the person to use drugs or other substances; withholding money or taking money from the person's purse without asking; taking the children away; refusing to take any part in helping with childcare or housework

- isolating: telling the other person where they can and cannot go; preventing them from seeing friends and relatives; shutting the person in the house; lying to the person's friends and family about them; monitoring or blocking telephone calls or disconnecting the telephone; being unreasonably jealous; having other relationships; breaking promises and shared agreements

- harassment: following or checking up on the other person; not allowing any privacy (for example, opening mail); checking to see who has telephoned the other person; accompanying them everywhere they go

- physical threats: making angry gestures; using physical size to intimidate; shouting the other person down; destroying their possessions; breaking things; punching walls; wielding a knife or a gun; threatening to kill or harm the other person and/or the children; threatening to harm family pets

- sexual violence: using force, threats or intimidation to make the other person perform sexual acts; having sex with the other person when they don't want it; forcing them to look at pornographic material; forcing them to have sex with other people; any degrading treatment related to the other person's sexuality or gender, whether they are lesbian, gay, bisexual or heterosexual, or transgender

- physical violence: punching; slapping; hitting; biting; pinching; kicking; pulling hair out; pushing; shoving; burning; strangling
- denial: saying the abuse doesn't happen; saying the other person caused the abusive behaviour; being publicly gentle and patient, whilst being abusive in private; crying and begging for forgiveness; saying it will never happen again.

Recognising when domestic abuse is happening to someone you know

For a huge range of reasons it can often be difficult for people with learning disabilities to find themselves a romantic partner. Some people may have very small social circles, and little choice of partners or examples of healthy relationships that they can follow. Some people may be so pleased to be in a relationship that they are prepared to put up with anything. They may not always realise that their partner is behaving abusively and that this is not how relationships should be. For these people it can be a challenge to make sense of what is happening, and they are unlikely to tell someone that they are being abused. Their upset and confusion may be expressed through a change in behaviour. They may self-harm, or behave inappropriately or harmfully towards others. There are many clues that you can pick up on if you are concerned that someone is experiencing domestic abuse. Below are some other signs:

- They may be withdrawing from social situations and from taking part in things outside the home, such as family get-togethers or their faith community.

- They may be defensive or over-protective when talking about their partner or family member.

- They may be short of money even when they should have more money available than they seem to.

- It may be difficult to make contact with them by phone.

- They may have unexplained injuries, or explain certain injuries in a way that doesn't make sense to you.

- They may have low self-esteem and seem anxious and less and less confident each time you see them.

If you suspect that someone that you know is a victim of domestic abuse, your moral support and your practical help will be extremely important. You may need to let them know that you are concerned about them in order for them to begin to confide in you. If a person tells you that they are experiencing domestic violence, then it is important to listen without judgement, and to understand that it takes a great deal of courage to talk about it because of the shame, humiliation, and fear they may be feeling. Reporting domestic abuse is a huge act of bravery for a victim. Never underestimate how much your support could help. Let the person know that there are resources that can help, and that you are available if they need to talk. Encourage the person to talk to the police, remember that there are often real risk implications for the person and it is important not to put them in any further danger by talking to their abuser yourself.

Safeguarding

If a child or an adult at risk tells you they have been a victim of abuse or that they are in danger, or if you have reason to believe they have been abused, you should report it to the police or to the local authority social services department.

Making decisions

Sometimes a person is not able to make a decision for themselves. This is called lacking capacity. Even if someone has capacity for everyday decisions, it doesn't mean that they will be a good judge around their personal safety. In England and Wales, the Mental Capacity Act explains how we can help someone to make a particular decision, if we think they may not be able to make it themselves. Those involved in the person's care and support, including family members, can ask for a 'best interest' meeting to help decide on the way forward. It can be so hard for someone who is used to being a victim to realise that they are being abused. The appointment of an IMCA (Independent Mental Capacity Advocate) by a social worker or care manager may be necessary. The Court of Protection also deals with issues like this on a regular basis, and can act quickly in urgent situations.

Reporting domestic abuse

Domestic abuse is a serious and violent crime. If you or someone you know is in immediate danger call 999 or 112. The police take domestic violence seriously and will be able to help and protect you or that person. If it is not an emergency but you want some support, you can contact your local neighbourhood policing team. The police should carry out a risk assessment and may introduce a police liaison officer.

The police liaison officer's priority is the person's safety, both now and in the future. They offer ongoing support and advice, and help keep the person (and if necessary their children) free from abuse.

Independent Domestic Violence Advocates (IDVA) can provide support and advice, letting the police concentrate on the investigation. An IDVA is an expert in keeping domestic abuse victims safe. The IDVA also works closely with all agencies involved in implementing each victim's safety plan and supporting them through the criminal justice process.

Some areas have Children's Independent Domestic Violence Advocates (KIDVA), who are specially trained to support children who are victims of domestic abuse.

Here are some of the actions the police, IDVA and other agencies can take to keep the person safe.

- Sanctuary schemes: this is when a safe room is created in a person's own home, by fitting new doors, locks and lighting. The person can use the room to call the police and wait in safety.

- Safeguarding the home: a Crime Prevention Tactical Advisor will visit and look at what can be done to help keep the person safe.

- Home alterations: the police can work with local councils to get security alterations made to the person's home, for example changing locks and fitting strong doors.

- Mobile phones: police can provide new mobile phones if people need a phone to keep safe.

- Address marker: police can put a special marker on a person's address so they know to come as quickly as possible when a call is made.

- Safety plans: if someone is living with domestic abuse they can get support to make a personal safety plan. This will help the person plan in advance how they will leave their home in an emergency. Police or an IDVA can help the person think about an escape plan, such as packing an emergency bag, hiding it somewhere safe, and drawing up a list of emergency phone numbers to carry with them.

- Moving home: if the person is a council tenant and needs to move, the police or IDVA can liaise with the local council to arrange this. They can also put the person in contact with organisations who can find them (and, if necessary, their children) a place at a refuge or safe house. Refuge addresses are always kept confidential.

- Support through court proceedings: if the abuser is taken to court, the police liaison officer or IDVA can talk the person through the court proceedings and arrange for them to give evidence behind a screen or via video link if they would prefer. If the person would rather not be in court, the police liaison officer or IDVA will make sure that they are told what happens.

What will happen to the victim and abuser?

The police's main concern will be the victim's safety. They will take what you say seriously, and respond quickly, especially if the domestic violence is occurring when you call. If you are a witness, police officers might ask you to give an oral and written account of what you heard or saw.

The perpetrator might be arrested, and then charged with a crime. Sometimes, the witness who called the police might be asked to come to court to testify about the events in front of the judge.

The simple act of calling the police about domestic abuse will help to protect the victim. As a witness, you should not have to worry that the perpetrator will hurt you or the victim in revenge. There are services in place to protect you both.

When an incident of domestic abuse is reported, a police officer will visit the victim either at home or somewhere they feel safe. The officer will talk to the victim about what has happened. Some of the questions may seem personal but the answers will help the police to understand the situation, and to develop a plan in partnership with the person to keep them safe. The officer may also take a statement.

With the victim's permission the police may also gather other evidence and take photographs of any injuries.

The police also have a responsibility to keep any children safe, and will share information with social services. The children will not be removed from the victim if they are not at risk from them.

If someone is arrested

Police officers take domestic abuse seriously. Although getting justice is important to them, officers consider each case and the wishes of people involved individually.

If someone is arrested they'll be taken to a police station. If they're charged with a crime, they may either be remanded into custody to appear before the next available court or released on bail while the police complete their investigation. They may be able to attach bail conditions to protect the victim from further abuse and intimidation. The court may also use Domestic Abuse Protection Orders or Notices, which are civil orders that give the victim short-term protection from their abuser, enabling the victim to focus on making plans and sorting out necessary things like childcare or somewhere to live.

If the abuser pleads guilty the victim won't have to go to court, but may be asked to give a victim impact statement describing the effect the abuse has had on them. The court will take this into account when passing sentence. If the abuser pleads not guilty the victim may have to go to court to give evidence. This is likely to raise anxiety, but arrangements can be made for the victim and any vulnerable witnesses to give evidence behind a screen or via video link so that they don't have to enter the court room and see their abuser.

Recovering from domestic abuse

When someone leaves a relationship where they have been experiencing domestic abuse, the most important first step is getting safe. Even once the abuse has stopped, and the abuser has faced legal sanctions, survivors will face many emotional and practical difficulties. It is important that people receive good support to help them make a new start.

Domestic abuse may leave a person with significant financial difficulties. This could be because money was controlled or misused by their partner, or because they have had to leave a job or another source of income and support. They may have had to leave a home situation quickly, leaving behind personal property and valuables. It is important that a survivor can get good financial advice, including advice about eligible benefits and grants, so that they can support themselves and any children.

Survivors may also need support with housing. Refuge housing is usually fixed-term, and shared. It provides safety, and often peer support and help to access services, but it is not a stable home. In the medium and longer term, people will need to find and establish a new place of their own.

Domestic abuse may affect a person's physical health too. Physical injuries, health conditions that have not been looked after properly, or poor diet and lifestyle can cause short or long-term health problems. Someone experiencing domestic abuse may not have seen a GP for some time. They may need time and supportive services to help them prioritise their physical health again.

Emotional recovery

One of the most significant long-term effects of domestic abuse may be on the mental health of the victim. Research indicates that the majority of women using mental health services have suffered some form of domestic abuse. Many may be dependent on alcohol or drugs and need to access services to support them to recover from that dependency. Even once their situation has stabilised, survivors may experience many difficult feelings:

- loss or grief
- anger
- loneliness
- lack of confidence
- low self-esteem
- anxiety
- depression.

If the person who has been abused has a learning disability or communication difficulty, they may express their pain in different ways, for example through behaviour which seems inappropriate, or which their supporters or friends find difficult to deal with. They may need support from a specialist psychotherapy service or Community Learning Disability Team to communicate about their experiences in a way that helps them begin to recover.

Lasting emotional support and often therapy, such as counselling, is crucial in helping any domestic abuse survivor to recover well.

In psychodynamic psychotherapy and counselling a therapeutic relationship is built up between client and therapist. This can be particularly important for people who have experienced abusive intimate relationships all their lives. The therapeutic relationship becomes a first chance to experience a trusting, safe relationship, and it can become a useful part of helping to support someone to change their relationship patterns. The therapy sessions also provide an opportunity for the person to discuss what is happening in their life, working out what is okay in their 'real life' relationships and what isn't, and to think about how they can bring about changes if they are unhappy with the way things are.

Building confidence for the future

One of the best ways to help people keep safe in relationships is to help them to build up their confidence and self-esteem. This can happen in a number of ways.

Getting active, taking up new hobbies or relearning old ones, and learning ways to relax and treat themselves well, can help increase a person's mental wellbeing and begin to change the way they think about their life. Learning new skills, like budgeting or work skills, can build self-esteem and also support independence and resilience in the future.

Group support can be very helpful to people who have experienced domestic abuse, creating opportunities to share experiences, as well as to talk about relationships and 'good' and 'bad' ways of treating one another. This book can be a good starting point to begin these kinds of discussions. Groups can engage in drama and role play to explore how people relate to one another and to work out the difference between unhealthy and healthy relationships. Role play can offer people the opportunity to try out ways of responding to different situations. This can be like a rehearsal so that it becomes easier to be assertive in real relationships.

If you or someone you know has survived domestic abuse, it may be hard to imagine a good and healthy relationship in the future, but these relationships can and do happen. If you are supporting someone with a learning disability, it is important not to protect them from the possibility of future relationships. They need to establish safe habits and a positive self-image that will help protect them in the long term, whether they are in a relationship or not.

Useful resources

The Global Foundation for the Elimination of Domestic Violence (EDV)

EDV Global Foundation is an NGO working to end domestic violence worldwide. EDV works with international organisations and at a governmental level to raise awareness of the problem, and a process of researching, designing and implementing programmes to tackle domestic violence in an effective way. EDV's website contains news and policy developments relating to the elimination of domestic violence.
www.gfedv.org

Services in the UK

Social services

Social services are provided by the local authority to ensure that adults and children receive the support they need to live well. They carry out social care assessments, requesting funding if someone needs social care support, including supported living or emergency rehousing, and reviewing that support. They will also lead on safeguarding proceedings if an adult or child is at risk of harm or abuse.

Respond

Respond works with children and adults with learning disabilities who have experienced abuse or trauma, as well as those who have abused others, through psychotherapy, advocacy, campaigning and other support. Respond also provides training, consultancy and research to combat abuse.
Helpline: 0808 808 0700
www.respond.org.uk

Beverley Lewis House
Beverley Lewis House is a supported housing service run by East Thames Group that safeguards women with learning disabilities and mental health issues or physical disabilities, who are at risk of, or fleeing abuse. Accommodation is provided for up to two years, and during this time residents are given help and support to recover from their abuse, develop new skills and interests and build confidence. Women can be referred to Beverley Lewis House by their social worker.
East Thames Group referral line: 0300 303 7333

National Centre for Domestic Violence (NCDV)
A free national service to help people who have suffered or are threatened with domestic violence to get an emergency injunction. The NCDV will help prepare statements, arrange court appearances, and refer people to legal aid or provide volunteers to draft injunction applications.
0844 8044 999 / 0800 970 2070
Or text NCDV to 60777 to receive a call back
www.ncdv.org.uk

Women's Aid
Women's Aid is a national charity aiming to stop domestic abuse via campaigning, education and services to women suffering abuse. Local member organisations provide direct support and services, such as outreach, refuge accommodation and training for schools and organisations.
www.womensaid.org.uk
To find your local Women's Aid organisation, visit the national website:
www.womensaid.org.uk/azrefuges.asp

Refuge
Refuge is a national charity providing direct services to women experiencing domestic abuse, via a network of safe houses. Women, and their children, are supported to recover from their abuse while living in safety, and to access further services, including legal advice, education and employment and a safe place to live. A number of culturally specific refuges are provided. Refuge also provides Independent Domestic Violence Advocates (IDVAs) to work with women at high risk from their abusers.
www.refuge.org.uk

National Domestic Violence Helpline
The freephone 24-hour National Domestic Violence Helpline is run in partnership between Women's Aid and Refuge. The helpline can provide emotional support, information, and referrals to emergency safe accommodation and other services.
0808 2000 247

The ManKind Initiative
A national charity that provides help and support for male victims of domestic abuse. ManKind runs a helpline for men experiencing abuse, and works to raise awareness and provide training for organisations working with male victims of domestic abuse.
Helpline: 01823 334244
www.mankind.org.uk

Men's Advice Line
A helpline for men experiencing abuse from a partner, ex-partner or family member, offering emotional and practical support and signposting to other services. The website also provides tools for working with men

who present as victims of domestic abuse.
Helpline: 0808 801 0327
www.mensadviceline.org.uk

Broken Rainbow
A national charity supporting lesbian, gay, bisexual and transgender victims of domestic abuse. Support is offered via a free confidential helpline, email and online chat.
Helpline: 0800 999 5428
Monday and Thursday 10am–8pm;
Tuesday and Wednesday 10am–5pm
help@brokenrainbow.org.uk
www.brokenrainbow.org.uk

Respect
A telephone and email service for people who are abusing their partners, offering support for them to stop. The website offers information about domestic abuse perpetrator programmes, and resources for working with domestic abuse perpetrators.
Respect phoneline: 0808 802 4040
Monday to Friday, 9am–5pm
info@respectphoneline.org.uk
www.respect.uk.net

Childline
Childline is a free 24-hour counselling service for children and young people up to 19. Counsellors can talk about any issue of concern, including domestic abuse that young people are suffering or witnessing. Support is available via phone, or by instant message and email through the Childline website.
Helpline: 0800 1111
www.childline.org.uk

Get connected
A free confidential support and signposting service for young people under 25. The service offers support via telephone, text, email and webchat, covering a variety of issues including domestic abuse.
Helpline: 0808 808 4994
text: 80849
www.getconnected.org.uk

Victim Support
Victim Support is a national charity supporting people affected by crime, including domestic abuse. People can be referred by the police or can refer themselves whether or not they report the crime and regardless of when the crime happened. Victim Support also operates a confidential helpline.
Victim Supportline: 0845 30 30 900
Monday to Friday 8am–8pm; weekends 9am–7pm
www.victimsupport.org.uk

Rape Crisis
An organisation supporting women and girls who have been the victim of sexual violence, outside or within a relationship. Rape Crisis has a network of local centres offering services such as counselling, advocacy, training and outreach. A national helpline is also available.
Helpline: 0808 802 9999
www.rapecrisis.org.uk

Against Forced Marriages
An organisation raising awareness and supporting communities where people are at risk of forced marriage. There is a freephone helpline for anyone who has concerns about themselves or another person.

Helpline: 0800 141 2994
www.againstforcedmarriages.org
Any urgent cases should be reported to the government **Forced Marriage Unit (FMU)**.
FMU: 020 7008 0151

Written materials and online resources

Don't Put Up With It! – Domestic Violence And Women With Learning Disabilities

A video produced following a two-year research project by Tizard Centre at the University of Kent Canterbury. The video explains the types of abuse women with learning disabilities may experience within relationships and how to get help.
https://vimeo.com/116967832

Bristol Against Violence and Abuse (BAVA)

www.bava.org.uk
BAVA has produced a teaching pack and video resource aimed specifically at people with learning disabilities. The video features members of Misfits Theatre acting out different domestic abuse scenarios, with opportunities for viewers to reflect on and discuss what they are seeing.
www.bava.org.uk/professionals/resources
The Spiralling video and toolkit on the same page is aimed at young people.

Equation

www.equation.org.uk
The Equation Project, formerly Nottinghamshire Domestic Violence Forum, offers some good interactive resources for young people to learn about what makes

healthy relationships, and to spot problems in their own relationships or relationships around them.
The GREAT Project is for children aged 9–11
www.thegreatproject.org.uk
Respect Not Fear is for young people aged 12–18
www.respectnotfear.co.uk

Can You See Me?
www.canyouseeme.coop
A video and educational resource produced by Women's Aid and the Midcounties Cooperative about relationships and abuse. There are resources and activities aimed at both young people and teachers, and a broad range of abusive behaviour is covered.

Easy Health
www.easyhealth.org.uk
An easy read website of resources about health and wellbeing topics, including abuse. All the linked leaflets and organisations are aimed at people with learning disabilities.

NICE public health guidance, *Domestic violence and abuse: how health services, social care and the organisations they work with can respond effectively*. This guidance sets out a number of recommendations for training and partnership working for services dealing with domestic violence.
www.nice.org.uk/guidance/ph50

Related titles in the Books Beyond Words series

Supporting Victims (2007) by Sheila Hollins, Kathryn Stone and Valerie Sinason, illustrated by Catherine Brighton. Polly is the victim of an assault. The book shows her experience as a witness at court, outlining the support and special measures that help her to give evidence.

When Dad Hurts Mum (2014) by Sheila Hollins, Patricia Scotland and Noëlle Blackman, illustrated by Anne-Marie Perks. After her dad is violent towards her mum, Katie is sad and distracted at college. Her teacher supports the family to get the help of an Independent Domestic Violence Advocate and the police. Katie and her mum are kept safe. Katie's dad is court-ordered to join a group to stop his abusive behaviour.

Jenny Speaks Out (2005, 2nd edition) by Sheila Hollins and Valerie Sinason, illustrated by Beth Webb. Jenny feels unsettled when she moves into a new home in the community. Her supporter and friends sensitively help Jenny to unravel her painful past as a victim of sexual abuse, and begin a slow but positive healing process.

Bob Tells All (1993) by Sheila Hollins and Valerie Sinason, illustrated by Beth Webb. Bob has moved to a group home, but his erratic behaviour and terrifying nightmares unsettle the other people living there. A social worker sensitively helps Bob unravel his painful past as a victim of sexual abuse. Bob discovers that talking with people he can trust begins a slow, but positive, healing process.

I Can Get Through It (2009, 2nd edition) by Sheila Hollins, Christiana Horrocks and Valerie Sinason, illustrated by Lisa Kopper. This book tells the story of a woman whose life is suddenly disturbed by an act of abuse. It shows how with the help of friends and counselling, the memory of the abuse slowly fades.

Mugged (2002) by Sheila Hollins, Christiana Horrocks and Valerie Sinason, illustrated by Lisa Kopper. This book tells the story of Charlie who is attacked in the street. The pictures show how Charlie is helped by speedy police action, Victim Support and back-up from friends, family and supporters.

Speaking Up For Myself (2002) by Sheila Hollins, Jackie Downer, Linette Farquarson and Oyepeju Raji, illustrated by Lisa Kopper. Having a learning disability and being from an ethnic minority group can make it hard to get good services. Natalie learns to fix problems by being assertive and getting help from someone she trusts.

Feeling Cross and Sorting it Out (2014) by Sheila Hollins and Nick Barratt, illustrated by Beth Webb. Ben doesn't like being rushed and when Paul won't make time for a chat, Ben gets cross and upset. Ben asks Jane for help and she helps them sort it out. Now Paul understands what is important for Ben and what has been worrying him. The story ends with them choosing a new activity to do together.

Authors and artist

Sheila Hollins is Emeritus Professor of Psychiatry of Disability at St George's, University of London, and sits in the House of Lords. She is a past President of the Royal College of Psychiatrists and of the BMA, and chairs the BMA's Board of Science. She is founding editor, author and Executive Chair of Books Beyond Words, and a family carer for her son who has a learning disability.

Patricia Scotland, Baroness Patricia Scotland of Asthal QC was the first female Attorney General for the UK. She has achieved several firsts: in 1991 aged thirty-five, she became the youngest woman ever to be appointed Queen's Counsel and was the first black woman appointed to the House of Lords. She is a committed activist in matters pertaining to legal reform, domestic violence and criminal justice, and is patron of the Global Foundation for the Elimination of Domestic Violence.

Noëlle Blackman is CEO of Respond, a charity which provides psychotherapy to people with learning disabilities who have experienced abuse or trauma. She has co-facilitated the GOLD (Growing Older with Learning Disabilities) group since 1998, and uses Books Beyond Words in her therapeutic practice. This is the fourth book she has co-authored with Baroness Hollins.

Anne-Marie Perks is an illustrator, visual artist and animator with published work in children's books. She has an MA in Children's Illustration from the North Wales School of Art and Design. Her paintings have won awards in exhibitions in the US and she frequently shows her work in the Society of Children's Book Writers' and Illustrators' touring exhibitions. Anne-Marie teaches illustration and animation at Buckinghamshire New University.

Acknowledgments

We thank our editorial advisers Deborah Jamieson and Gary Butler.

We are grateful for the advice and support of our advisory group, which included representatives from Global Federation for the Elimination of Domestic Violence, Respond, Bromley Sparks, Beverley Lewis House, Tizard Centre, STORM Empowerment, Wandsworth Psychological Therapies & Wellbeing Service: John Phillips, Sylv Hibbit, Gillian Rees, Sue Langley, Jenny Cashman, Asha Jama, Michelle McGovern, Michelle McCarthy, Marie Hanson, Tina Cowles, Mavis Dwaah.

We are also grateful to all the people who read earlier drafts of the picture story, including members of Beverley Lewis House, Bromley Sparks, St Joseph's Specialist School and College, Tizard Centre Domestic Violence Focus Group, Researchnet Group: Linda Allchorne, Joanne Gifford, Teresa Durman, Carol Larby, Polly Sharpey, Laura Frewin, Abigail Edler, Charlotte Cranidge, Julie Anderson, Cas Anstee.

Finally we are very grateful to the Department of Health for providing financial support for this book.

Beyond Words: publications and training

Books Beyond Words are stories for anyone who finds pictures easier than words. A list of all Beyond Words publications, including print and eBook versions of Books Beyond Words titles, and where to buy them, can be found on our website:

www.booksbeyondwords.co.uk

Workshops for family carers, support workers and professionals about using Books Beyond Words are provided regularly in London, or can be arranged in other localities on request. Self-advocates are welcome. For information about forthcoming workshops see our website or contact us:

email: admin@booksbeyondwords.co.uk
tel: 020 8725 5512

Video clips showing our books being read are also on our website and YouTube channel: www.youtube.com/user/booksbeyondwords and on our DVD, *How to Use Books Beyond Words*.